THE COMPLETE BOOK OF
AURAS

ABOUT THE AUTHOR

Author of more than forty titles published with Llewellyn, Richard Webster is one of New Zealand's most prolific writers. His best-selling books include *Spirit Guides & Angel Guardians, Creative Visualization for Beginners, Soul Mates, Is Your Pet Psychic?, Practical Guide to Past-Life Memories, Astral Travel for Beginners, Miracles*, and the four-book series on archangels: *Michael, Gabriel, Raphael*, and *Uriel*.

A noted psychic, Richard is a member of the National Guild of Hypnotherapists (USA), the Association of Professional Hypnotherapists and Parapsychologists (UK), the International Registry of Professional Hypnotherapists (Canada), and the Psychotherapy and Hypnotherapy Institute of New Zealand. When not touring, he resides in New Zealand with his wife and family.

THE COMPLETE BOOK OF
AURAS

Learn to See, Read, Strengthen & Heal Auras

RICHARD WEBSTER

Llewellyn Publications
Woodbury, Minnesota

First Edition, 2010
First Printing, 2010

Cover design by Kevin R. Brown
Cover photo © iStockphoto.com/Ron Chapple Studios
Interior illustration by Llewellyn art department

Llewellyn is a registered trademark of Llewellyn Worldwide Ltd.

Library of Congress Cataloging-in-Publication Data
Webster, Richard, 1946–
   The complete book of auras : learn to see, read, strengthen & heal auras / Richard Webster.—1st ed.
       p. cm.
   Includes bibliographical references (p.   ) and index.
   ISBN 978-0-7387-2180-4
   1. Aura. I. Title.
   BF1389.A8W44 2010
   133.8'92—dc22
                                    2010032713

Llewellyn Publications
A Division of Llewellyn Worldwide Ltd.
2143 Wooddale Drive
Woodbury, MN 55125-2989
www.llewellyn.com

Printed in the United States of America

For two special friends,
TC Tahoe and Lesley Lange

ALSO BY RICHARD WEBSTER

CONTENTS

INTRODUCTION

WHEN I STARTED working, my first boss had a reputation in the company for always knowing when a female staff member became pregnant. He would tell the men in the cafeteria about it whenever this occurred, and we'd all wait expectantly to see if he was correct. He always was. A week, or a month, or even later, the young woman would announce that she was pregnant, only to be told by everyone that they already knew. After witnessing this several times, I asked him how he did it. He replied that pregnant women emit a special glow that he could instantly recognize.

"I see it all the time," he told me. "Whenever I walk down a street I look at the young women. I can tell if they're sad, happy, in love, or pregnant, purely from the glow around their faces. It's easy—anyone can do it."

Although my boss would have been surprised to hear it, he was seeing the auras of these young women. To the best of my knowledge, his interest in the subject never went beyond determining whether or not someone was pregnant, but he obviously had developed some degree of aura consciousness.

Once you gain aura awareness, you'll be able to do everything my former boss did, and much more. The ability to see and sense auras will enhance your life in many ways and enable you to help others more than ever before.

Throughout history, certain people have been able to see auras. Possibly the earliest depictions of these can be seen in the ancient rock carvings in the Val Camonica region of Northern Italy. These show people who seem to be wearing a strange type of headgear. Some people claim that this proves that beings from other planets visited Earth thousands of years ago. However, as some of these drawings show what appear to be flames surrounding the head, it is more likely that they are depictions of people's auras.

There are at least three occurrences in the Bible that appear to relate to auras. When Moses descended from the mountain holding the tablets containing the Ten Commandments, his followers noticed something different about him. "And when Aaron and all the children of Israel saw Moses, behold, the skin of his face shone; and they were afraid to come nigh him" (Exodus 34:30). At the Transfiguration of Christ, Matthew recorded that Jesus' "face did shine as the sun, and his raiment was white as the light" (Matthew 17:2). When Saul, later to become St. Paul, was on the road to Damascus, "suddenly there shined round about him a light from heaven" (Acts 9:3).

Well before Christian artists started depicting halos around saints, martyrs, and angels, artists in ancient Egypt, Greece, Rome, and India encircled their most spiritually evolved people with halos to show the sacred nature of their subjects. Sacred books from the same period also mention auras.

Hildegard von Bingen (1098–1179) was arguably the first person in the West to write about auras, when she described the luminous sights she saw in her visions. There are many accounts of auras in Christian, particularly Catholic, writings. In the fourteenth century, when John Tornerius, a Carthusian priest, failed to attend Mass, a sacristan went to his cell and reported that the room was radiant with a luminous light that emanated from the Father. On one occasion, the light emanating from the Blessed Giles of Assisi was so great, that it totally eclipsed the light of the moon.[1]

In the sixteenth century, Paracelsus (1493–1541), the Swiss physician and alchemist, described the aura as a "fiery globe." He wrote: "The vital force is not enclosed in man, but radiates round him like a luminous sphere, and it may be able to act at a distance. In these semi-natural rays the imagination of man may produce healthy or morbid effects. It may poison the essence of life and cause diseases, or it may purify it after it has been made impure, and restore the health."[2]

One hundred years later, Johann Baptista van Helmont (1580–1644), a Flemish physician and chemist, put forward the theory that human beings radiated a magnetic fluid called *magnale magnum*. He believed this could be utilized for healing purposes. He also believed in the existence of the soul, which he called *aura vitalis seminum*.

Emmanuel Swedenborg (1688–1772), the Swedish mystic and scientist, described the aura in his *Spiritual Diary*: "There is a spiritual sphere surrounding every one, as well as a natural and corporal one."

In 1845, Baron Karl von Reichenbach (1788–1869), an Austrian scientist who discovered paraffin and creosote, described an energy that he called *od*, or *odic force*. He found that certain sensitive people were able to see a faint light emanating from the poles of a magnet. This led him to further experiments in darkened rooms using specially chosen subjects that he called *sensitives*. His test subjects reported seeing sparks, rays of light and flame-like energy emitted from fingertips, plants, animals, magnets and specific crystals. Despite the constant criticism his research provoked, Baron von Reichenbach continued researching and publishing his findings until his death.

In 1908, Dr. Walter J. Kilner (1847–1920), an English doctor, found that the human aura could be seen if viewed through a screen containing dicyanin, a coal-tar dye. Dicyanin made the person temporarily shortsighted and this enabled him or her to see the radiation present in the ultraviolet part of the spectrum. Using the screen, Dr.

Kilner, and anyone else interested, could see the size, color, and texture of the different layers of the aura. Dr. Kilner also experimented with a variety of gaseous vapors, such as ammonia, bromine, chlorine, and iodine, to see how they affected the aura. Some changed the color of the aura while others caused the innermost layer to contract. Dr. Kilner even found volunteers who could voluntarily change the color of their auras. They were able to affect the entire aura or any part of it that he cared to name.

Even more importantly, Dr. Kilner studied the auras of healthy people in addition to people suffering from different illnesses. As a result of his research, he became convinced that he could accurately identify both healthy and unhealthy auras. He wrote: "Examination of their aura has been the means of reassuring not a few people who had come up under the impression that they were suffering from cancer."[3]

Dr. Kilner published a book about his findings, *The Human Aura*, in 1911, and was ridiculed by the medical establishment as a result. Fortunately, this did not deter him. He continued researching and his final book, *The Human Atmosphere*, was published in 1921. Using dicyanin, Dr. Kilner discerned three layers to the aura. The first, called the etheric double, was a fine, almost transparent layer closest to the body. It is approximately one-fourth to one-half an inch wide. Surrounding this is the inner aura, which is dense and extends about three inches from the person, and the outer aura, which contracts and expands, extending almost twelve inches from the body. He noticed healthy people emitted rays of colors that came from the body and headed to the outer aura. As unhealthy people did not have these, Dr. Kilner began studying the aura to see if it could be used to diagnose illnesses.

The remarkable factor in Dr. Kilner's research is that he had no knowledge or interest in the occult. He had not read anything on Eastern mysticism or Theosophy. Despite this, his scientific approach produced the same findings that mystical people had described for thousands of years.

Oscar Bagnall, an English biologist, continued Dr. Kilner's research, and developed a screen containing pinacynol and methalene blue. These screens could be worn as spectacles and were popularly known as "aura goggles." Special glasses that enable people to see auras are still available on the Internet today. Oscar Bagnall's book on the subject, *The Origin and Properties of the Human Aura* was published in 1937.

In the twentieth century, people became interested in photographing auras. However, the Schlieren device, a nineteenth-century invention to detect flaws in glass, was the first device able to photograph auras. It shows what has been described as a "shimmering, rainbow-colored aura"[4] surrounding people. Doctors at the City University of London examined these energies surrounding the body and discovered it contained more than 400 percent more microorganisms than the surrounding air. This led them to theorize that the "aura" contained potential diseases because the warm air effectively trapped bacteria, as well as inorganic matter and small pieces of discarded skin.[5] Most aura readers believe disease can be seen in the etheric body, the part of the aura closest to the skin, and these photographs appear to confirm that.

In 1939, Semyon Davidovich Kirlian (1898–1978), a Russian electronics engineer, accidentally discovered he could photograph auras. His first insight came when he watched a patient receiving electric shock treatment at a psychiatric institution. He noticed a tiny flash of light between the patient's skin and an electrode. After making this discovery he, with his wife Valentina, built a camera that ran electric current from a high-frequency spark-generator over plates that held a sheet of photographic film. Semyon Kirlian burned his hand when he first tried it, but the pain was quickly forgotten when he saw a photograph of his auric field on the photographic plate. The luminescent photographs that this simple camera produced showed auras around all living things.

On one occasion, a Soviet official gave them two virtually identical leaves and requested photographs of them. The Kirlians were delighted to have the opportunity to show how well their device worked. They spent the whole night taking photographs to ensure the official received the best possible results. However, no matter how hard they tried, only one of the leaves produced the bright luminescent effect they were trying to obtain. One leaf revealed spherical flares in a symmetrical formation over the whole leaf. The other leaf produced just a few dark shapes. Their disappointment vanished when the official told them that one of the plants had been contaminated with a serious disease, which their camera had picked up.[6]

The Kirlians spent thirteen years studying Kirlian photography before the Soviet authorities provided them with a modern laboratory to continue their work.

Later researchers have continued to explore Kirlian photography, particularly in the field of health. One of the most notable researchers is Dr. Valerie Hunt, who was a professor of kinesiology at UCLA for thirty-five years. In her book, *Infinite Mind: Science of Human Vibrations of Consciousness*, she wrote: "As a result of my work, I can no longer consider the body as organic systems or tissues. The healthy body is a flowing, interactive electrodynamic energy field."[7]

At the Neuropsychiatric Institute of the University of California in Los Angeles, Dr. Thelma Moss (1918–1997) researched the correlation between people's emotional states and the colored flashes that appear at their fingertips in Kirlian photographs. She discovered that people displaying strong emotions, such as anger, produced red coronas at their fingertips, but relaxed and contented people produced blue coronas. Another fascinating finding occurred occasionally when fingertips of two people were photographed at the same time. Every now and again, one person's corona disappeared. The scientists hypothesized that occasionally the energy fields of more dominant personalities were able to overshadow the energy fields of less dominant people.[8]

In the late 1980s, Dr. Harry Oldfield, a British homeopath, developed his own imaging system based on the Kirlians' research. He called his system Polycontrast Interference Photography (PIP). His camera records the energy fields surrounding people's bodies to determine their states of health. If a problem is found, Dr. Oldfield endeavors to heal the patient by rebalancing the energy surrounding him or her. Not surprisingly, Dr. Oldfield's claims have received a great deal of skepticism, and research is still ongoing.[9]

Aura imaging cameras can be found in many New Age shows, shopping malls, and exhibitions around the world. They serve a valuable purpose in introducing people to auras. Unfortunately, though, these cameras do not photograph the actual aura. Instead, they read it electronically and convert the energy into colors that reflect the person's feelings and emotional state at the time the photograph is taken. Usually, the person having his or her aura photograph taken sits in front of a plain background and places one hand on a sensor plate that picks up emanations from the person, which are translated by the computer and converted into a colorful swirl of colors surrounding a photograph of the person. The colors that appear can give indications as to the person's personality, but more commonly reveal the moods and emotions of the person at the time.

In 2009, researchers in Japan used special cameras capable of detecting single photons to examine the light emitted from the human body. This light is one thousand times lower than the levels our naked eyes can detect. Over three days, five healthy young male volunteers were photographed in total darkness every three hours from 10:00 a.m. to 10:00 p.m. The researchers discovered that the emanation rose and fell during the day. It was lowest at 10:00 a.m. and reached its peak at 4:00 p.m. After that, it gradually declined. Because the fluctuations of this light are likely to be connected to the person's metabolic rhythms, this form of photography shows potential for detecting imbalances and medical conditions in the human body.[10]

Research into the subject is ongoing, and it's an area where people can still do original research. I hope that after reading this book, you'll be sufficiently motivated and inspired to carry on your own explorations into this fascinating subject.

In this book you'll learn how to feel and see auras. You'll discover how to use your aura to obtain good health, a powerful faith, and success in every area of your life. Knowledge of auras can help you set and achieve your goals. You'll discover the amazing chakra system, the powerful batteries that energize your entire being. You'll learn how to give aura readings for others. You'll also learn how to use your knowledge of auras to help yourself and others.

1

WHAT IS THE AURA?

ACCORDING TO THE dictionary, the aura is an electromagnetic energy field that surrounds all living things. Ursula Roberts called it "a magnetic field of vibration which surrounds every person, in the same way that light surrounds a lighted candle or perfume surrounds a flower."[1] In his book, *The Human Aura*, Swami Panchadasi described the aura as "a fine, ethereal radiation or emanation surrounding each and every living human being. It extends from two to three feet, in all directions, from the body."[2] In fact, the aura is much more than this. As it is part of every cell in the body, the aura is more correctly described as an extension of the body, rather than something that surrounds it.

The aura reveals the person's character, mental and emotional state, health, vitality, and path through life. Habitual thoughts and emotions are clearly revealed in the aura. If the person changes his or her long-standing thoughts and emotions, the aura will also change to reflect that. People who read auras can tell exactly how you're feeling about life at any given moment, because it's revealed clearly in your aura.

The aura of the average person is roughly egg shaped and extends eight to ten feet away from the body in all directions. Some highly spiritual people are said to have had auras that extended several miles, and their followers enjoyed spending time with them partly because they could sense the person's aura surrounding them. Some of Gautama Buddha's early followers claimed that his aura extended 200 miles.[3]

The aura retracts and expands in size depending on the health and vitality of the person. Someone who is enthusiastic, physically fit, and full of the joys of life will have a much larger aura than someone who is frail and negative. The person with the larger aura is better protected from outside forces than the person with an aura that hugs his or her body. The person with the larger aura will enjoy life much more and will feel in control. The person with the smaller aura, on the other hand, will feel helpless, tired, and ineffective.

Your aura is constantly interacting with the auras of the people you meet everywhere you go. Your aura is expanding and contracting all the time as a result of your interactions with positive and negative people, and the people you like and dislike. You, and they, are constantly absorbing and passing out energy. This is why you feel depleted and drained of energy after spending time with negative people. I'm sure you know people who always leave you feeling absolutely exhausted, as they've drained all the energy from your aura. This is usually done subconsciously, but I've met a few people who deliberately strengthen their auras by depleting others. These people are called psychic vampires.

Conversely, you also know people who you enjoy spending time with because they make you feel good. They have energy to spare and subconsciously help you expand your aura. Spending time with friends and loved ones also produces the same effect.

Consequently, everywhere you go, you interact with people who affect your aura, for good or ill. Fortunately, there are a number of ways to strengthen and expand your aura when necessary, and we'll discuss them later.

The word *aura* comes from the Greek word *avra*, which means air or a breeze. Thousands of years ago, clairvoyants noticed that our auras continually flow and change depending on our moods, emotions, health, mental state, and level of spiritual awareness.

Auras contain all the colors of the spectrum. They can also change color to reflect people's moods and emotions. If someone is "in the pink," he or she is likely to be in love, and pink will be extremely obvious in the aura. Someone who is "green with envy," "feeling blue," or "red with rage" cannot hide his or her mood from anyone who can see auras. Someone in the depths of despair is said to be in a "black hole." Someone who is "black-hearted" may well be caught "red-handed." A coward is called "yellow." All of these expressions came about because people observed these colors in people's auras and found they were consistently correct.

Children seem to instinctively know which colors reflect different moods. This is not surprising, as many young children see auras around the people they love and can tell if Mommy or Daddy is happy, sad, or angry. Often this aura awareness is revealed in their art. Unfortunately, many parents unintentionally close down this ability by making comments, such as, "Why did you draw your brother red?" The child might be drawing his or her brother's aura, which in this case, happened to be red. After hearing questions of this sort a number of times, most children stop drawing the energy fields, as they think their teachers and parents don't approve. It's a fortunate child who receives encouragement when drawing these energy fields.

Auras change in size and intensity according to the feelings of the person they surround. Someone who is eagerly waiting for his or her lover to arrive will reveal a vibrant, excited, and large aura. Someone who is feeling unwell or depressed will have a small aura with lackluster colors. However, if that person won the Lotto, the aura would immediately expand and the colors would become vibrant to reveal the sudden energy and happiness the person experienced on hearing the news.

That's because the aura is changing all the time to reveal what is going on in the person's life, moment by moment. Thoughts and emotions have an immediate effect on our bodies and auras.

Not long ago, I visited my doctor for a checkup. He commented that my heart rate was higher than normal. I wasn't aware that I'd been feeling nervous about the visit, but my body knew, and my doctor was able to pick this up. A few minutes later, he checked me again and my heart rate had returned to normal. This was because I'd told myself to relax, and my heart rate immediately dropped. In this instance, my body was aware of feelings I didn't know I had, and this caused my heart rate to rise. When I deliberately thought relaxing thoughts, it dropped again. These feelings would also have been reflected in my aura.

Every thought gives off a vibration that can be measured. Passing thoughts create small vibrations, while powerful thoughts, powered by emotion or desire, create strong vibrations that can be clearly seen in the aura.

The aura consists of several layers known as subtle bodies. Most people can, with practice, feel at least three of these. However, many healers and people who are highly intuitive can feel the other layers, even if they can't see them.

In the past, people thought each layer related to a different aspect of life. There are three main layers: the etheric double, the astral body, and the mental body. The astral body looks after the emotions, while the mental body governs thought. Nowadays, we know that thoughts can affect our emotions, and vice versa. As a result, most people look at the aura as a whole, rather than examine each layer separately.

Many clairvoyants claim the aura has seven layers:

1. The Physical Etheric Plane

2. The Astral Plane

3. The Lower Mental Plane

4. The Higher Mental Plane

5. The Spiritual Plane

6. The Intuitional Plane

7. The Absolute Plane

They relate these to the seven chakras, which are energy centers inside the aura. Although I can sometimes feel some of these layers, in practice I look at the aura as a whole.

However, there is one exception to this. The etheric double is an extremely fine, virtually invisible layer that extends between a quarter and half inch all around the body. It expands while the person is asleep, and contracts when the person is awake. Because of this, it appears to be a type of battery that recharges itself overnight.

When people start seeing auras, they usually see the etheric double as a space between the physical body and the aura. However, as their auric sight develops, they realize that the etheric double has a grayish tinge, and constantly shimmers, moves, and even changes color. This movement creates a wide variety of almost luminous colors that appear delicate and constantly change.

The etheric double is sometimes known as the health aura, as illnesses can be seen inside it as a dark smudge or a break in the movements of the aura. Ill health is also indicated by a loss of color in the etheric double. Illnesses can usually be seen in the etheric double well before the person is aware that something is wrong. This can be extremely useful—if people are made aware of potential problems they can take steps to restore their health before anything goes badly wrong.

Thoughts also affect the etheric double. Someone who constantly thinks negative thoughts will have a dull etheric double compared to the beautiful, radiant one that someone who thinks mainly positive thoughts will have.

Surrounding the etheric double are the different layers of the aura. Some people see these layers as sheathes, and in the East they are known as *koshas*, which not surprisingly means "sheath."

HOW TO DEVELOP AWARENESS
OF THE DIFFERENT LAYERS

This exercise will help you become aware of your mental, emotional, and physical bodies. You will need approximately thirty minutes to perform this exercise. Make sure you will not be disturbed, and that the room is reasonably warm. The exercise involves eleven steps:

1. Sit or lie down comfortably on your back. Close your eyes, and take three slow, deep breaths. Allow yourself to relax. Think about your physical body and how it tirelessly works for you. Touch and feel your body. You might stroke your stomach and chest. Gently examine your face, arms, and legs. For a minute or two, appreciate your magnificent body and everything it does for you, day after day.

2. When you feel ready, place your hands by your sides. Take several slow, deep breaths, and then gradually allow all the muscles of your body to relax. I normally start with my toes, and gradually work my way up to the top of my head. Another method is to tense different parts of your body for a few moments, and then let go. This causes the muscles to relax. Another useful method is to visualize the number 100 in your mind. Concentrate until you can clearly see it. Once you can see it clearly, allow it to fade away and be replaced by the number 99. Make this number as clear as you can, and then let it fade away. Continue counting down until it becomes too much effort to continue. By this stage your physical body will be completely relaxed.

3. Become aware of your physical body, and think about your different internal organs, such as your heart, lungs, stomach, and kidneys. In your imagination, feel them in the same way you did when you stroked and touched your body. It makes no difference if you don't know their exact size, shape, or position. Simply feel them in your mind, and appreciate them for everything they do for you.

4. Take a slow, deep breath and forget about your physical body. Think about your emotions, and allow yourself to feel them. Think about something that upset or annoyed you in the recent past. Allow yourself to experience the feelings in your body that this experience created. Notice any changes in your body as you relive this experience. You might notice a sensation of tightness in your stomach. There could be changes in your blood flow, and you might feel tension in your body.

5. Take another slow, deep breath and let go of that experience. Replace it with an exciting, rewarding, or happy incident from your recent past. Again, relive this incident recalling all the details. Notice any changes in your body as you relive this scene. You may feel a sense of excitement. You may find yourself smiling. You may notice something in the area of your heart.

6. Take a slow, deep breath and focus your attention on your heart. Allow feelings of love to flow through your entire body. Notice any feelings or sensations in the area of your heart.

7. Take another slow, deep breath, and this time pay attention to your thoughts. We all have some fifty to sixty thousand thoughts a day, most of them random. For a minute or two, try not to evaluate any thoughts that come into your mind. Simply let them come and go, and move in any direction they wish.

8. When you feel ready to move on, focus on a thought as it passes through your mind. Examine it, and deliberately change that thought into something else.

9. Take a slow, deep breath and lie comfortably, thinking about the meditation you are about to finish. In this calm, peaceful, relaxed state, you can see that you are much, much more than a physical body. You have experienced the effects that your thoughts and emotions have on your physical body. You have

seen that you can deliberately change your thoughts. Consequently, although you can't see it, you possess an emotional body and a mental body, in addition to your physical body. You have also experienced an outpouring of love in the area of your heart. This is a chakra position, which we'll discuss later. The chakras play an important part in the effective functioning of your subtle bodies.

10. Remain in this quiet, peaceful state for a minute or two. You might like to repeat some of the stages again to experience the different sensations they provide.

11. When you feel ready, take three slow, deep breaths and open your eyes. Lie still for a minute or two, and then get up. You will find it helpful to eat or drink something after this exercise, as this helps to ground you again.

THE COLORS IN THE AURA

The first time you see an aura it will probably seem to be white and almost cloudlike in appearance. Gradually, with practice you'll start to see colors. Every aura has a basic color that reveals important information about the person, as it reveals his or her emotional, mental, and spiritual nature.

In addition to this, the aura contains rays of different colors that emanate outward from the body. These radiating rays are sometimes said to be thought waves, as our thoughts and emotions have a major effect on the aura. These thought waves come and go, and are not a permanent part of the aura. This is probably fortunate, as no one would want to be permanently red with rage or green with envy.

Our auras interact all the time with the auras of the people we come into contact with throughout the day. When you meet someone you like, your aura will open up and the two auras will intermingle. In fact, when two people are deeply in love, their auras appear to combine, creating a huge, vibrantly beautiful aura. Of course, you may not like or love everyone you meet. If you dislike someone, your aura and the other person's aura will repel each other. This can happen instantly. If you instantly dislike someone for no apparent reason, it will be reflected in both auras. Your aura will dominate some people's auras, it will merge with the auras of people you like, and repel the auras of people you don't. It is doing this all the time.

Have you ever noticed how the energy of a room can change instantly when a certain person walks in? This is because his or her aura is affecting the auras of everyone else in the room. Have you ever met someone and instantly liked them? Again, this is because the two auras were attracted to each other.

The aura is not present at the moment of birth, but starts to appear with the baby's first breath.[4] This suggests that the aura consists of energy that is absorbed into the body by the breath and then radiated back out again as the aura.

A baby's aura is virtually colorless, but gains a silvery hue by the time he or she is three months old. The silver gradually changes to blue, indicating the development of intelligence. This usually occurs between the ages of one and two. At the same time a yellow haze appears around the head, indicating the start of thought. This haze becomes brighter and more intense as the child continues to learn and think. Naturally, the aura grows along with the child. As it develops, it indicates the child's potentials, and the permanent colors start to appear. They will be obvious by the time he or she starts school. The blue remains as a background color that is usually noticeable only when the child is unwell. This blue slowly fades away as the child grows.

Every aura should be large, radiant, and glowing with energy, enthusiasm, and good health. However, this is seldom the case. An average person will have an average aura. It will grow temporarily, and appear more beautiful, if he or she is being generous. Someone who is naturally good, kind, and generous will have a large aura with beautiful colors that look as if they've been drawn with pastels.

In the next chapter you'll gain further aura awareness by learning how to sense and feel the aura.

2

HOW TO FEEL AND SENSE THE AURA

SOME PEOPLE ARE able to see auras spontaneously, without any training or practice. However, they are very much in the minority. Most people need to start by feeling and sensing the aura. Once they can do that, seeing the aura is the logical next step.

The best way to gain aura awareness is to find someone to work with. This person needs to be just as keen as you are to develop their aura awareness. Do not choose someone simply because they are available. People who are not genuinely interested will quickly lose interest and their negativity will adversely affect you. This is why it is usually better to choose a friend rather than a family member to help you. Someone in your family might volunteer to help you out of a sense of duty, even though they're not interested.

Take your time and choose someone you like. You may have a friend or acquaintance who is interested in the subject. Alternatively, you might meet someone at a psychic development class, in a New Age bookstore, or Spiritualist Church.

Someone who attended one of my classes many years ago told me that she placed small flyers in books on auras at her local library. Her flyers asked people who were interested in learning more about auras to contact her. She heard from three or four people and they met once a week to practice and develop their skills. I thought this was a good idea, but suggest you ask people to contact you first by email. It's potentially dangerous to put your name and phone number inside library books, as you have no idea who may pick them up.

Once you've found the right person, it's time to start feeling the aura.

DOWSING THE AURA

Dowsing is the art of finding something that is hidden. Most people assume dowsers spend their time searching for underground water, but dowsing can be used to find almost anything, including gold, oil, and even missing people. Dowsing is extremely old. A pictograph in the Tassili-n-Ajjer caves in southeast Libya show a group of people watching a dowser with a forked stick. These paintings are approximately 8,000 years old.[1]

You can make your own angle rods using two pieces of wire approximately eighteen inches long. I made my first dowsing rods from coat hanger wire, and they served me well for many years. Once you have two pieces of wire, you need to bend them at right angles about six inches from one end. The angle wires are held loosely in the hands by the six-inch sections, while the twelve-inch sections face forward. Many dowsers cover the shorter section with plastic or wood tubing. Plastic straws work well, too. These allow the rods to move freely, no matter how tightly the dowser is holding the tubes. I used the shells of two ballpoint pens for my first angle rods. Some dowsers prefer to hold the rods loosely in their hands as they feel the rods move too freely inside a tube. This is a matter of personal preference, and you should experiment to see which method you prefer.

You will need to practice with your angle rods before dowsing for someone's aura. The easiest way to do this is to go outside and dowse for the water mains that enter your home. Start on one side of your property, with your angle rods pointing straight ahead. Relax your mind as much as you can. Tell yourself that you are dowsing for water and slowly walk from one side of your property to the other. At some stage, your angle rods will start to cross over each other and will become parallel to each other in front of you. With some people, the dowsing rods will move outward, away from each other, and the rods will indicate left and right. Both of these possibilities are known as the dowsing response. The rods will have crossed over each other as you walked over the water pipe. This may seem strange and unreal at first, but repetition will prove its accuracy. The key to success is to suspend disbelief, relax, and think of what you are dowsing for (in this case water).

Once you have become familiar with the dowsing response, you can dowse for your friend's aura. Ask your friend to stand with his or her arms and legs slightly apart. Stand about thirty feet away with your dowsing rods pointing forward. You can approach from any angle, but it is usually easier to dowse from behind the person, especially when you are both starting to experiment. Relax, and tell yourself that you are dowsing for your friend's aura. Move slowly toward your friend until the angle rods start to move. Pause for a few seconds, and then move forward even more slowly until the angle rods cross each other. This indicates the outer edge of your friend's aura.

Make a mental note of this position, and then repeat the exercise from the person's front and sides. You will discover that his or her aura extends an equal distance in all directions. In fact, if you now walk slowly around your friend while watching the tips of your angle rods, you'll find that his or her aura makes a perfect circle.

Change places, and allow your friend to dowse for your aura. If possible, dowse for other people's auras as well. You'll probably be surprised at how large people's auras are. This is because you're dowsing the outer edge of the aura. When you start feeling people's auras you're more likely to feel an inner layer.

HOW TO FEEL YOUR OWN AURA

The first parts of this exercise can be done on your own, as you'll be feeling your own aura. You need to be completely relaxed in both mind and body. Make sure the room you'll be experimenting in is pleasantly warm, and that you will not be disturbed for at least thirty minutes. You might want to temporarily disconnect the phone.

Sit down in a comfortable chair, close your eyes and take three slow, deep breaths. Hold each breath for a few seconds before exhaling. Once you've done this, allow the muscles in your toes and feet to relax. Once they feel completely relaxed, relax the muscles in your calves, knees, and thighs. Gradually relax all the muscles in your body until you feel totally relaxed.

Enjoy the feelings of pleasant relaxation. Recall some of the happiest moments in your life, and realize that you are perfect as you are. You are a worthwhile human being, making the most of this incarnation.

When you feel ready, open your eyes and stretch your arms and legs. The purpose of what you've just done is to become relaxed, focused, and in the right frame of mind to feel your own aura.

Start by briskly rubbing your hands together for several seconds, and then hold them about twelve inches apart with the palms facing each other. You may feel some energy in the fingertips and palms of your hands.

Slowly move your hands toward each other. You will gradually become aware of a slight resistance as the auras from each hand meet. Most people find it helpful to imagine that they're squashing a rubber ball between their hands. However, you might feel it in a different way. You might experience a slight resistance, a tingling sensation, or even a feeling of warmth or coolness.

Continue bringing your hands together until the two palms touch each other. You will find that the slight resistance disappears as the two auras merge together.

Hold your palms together for a few moments, and then slowly draw them apart. You'll notice a fine coolness on your palms and fingertips as the auras separate again.

Repeat this exercise until you can feel the aura. Everyone is different. Some people feel their aura on the first try, but others need to persevere until they can feel it. Once you've done it once, you'll have no difficulty in feeling your aura any time you wish.

Once you've succeeded, experiment further by moving your hands a couple of inches toward and away from each other. You'll notice a slight resistance as they move together, and a sense of coolness as they separate.

HOW TO FEEL YOUR CHAKRAS

Inside your aura are a number of energy centers, known as chakras. We'll be discussing these in chapter 4. The chakras absorb and distribute physical, mental, emotional, and spiritual energies. The seven most important chakras are situated alongside the spinal column, and can be easily felt with your hands.

The seven chakras are:

1. The Root chakra, which is situated at the base of the spine.

2. The Sacral chakra, which is situated halfway between the pubic bone and the navel.

3. The Solar Plexus chakra, which is situated at the level between the navel the sternum.

4. The Heart chakra, which is situated between the shoulder blades in line with the heart.

5. The Throat chakra, which is situated at the level of the throat.

6. The Brow chakra, which is situated at the level of the forehead, immediately above the eyebrows.

7. The Crown chakra, which is situated at the top of the head.

With practice, you'll be able to find and feel all seven of these chakras. Once you've succeeded, you'll be amazed that you weren't aware of them before, because once you become familiar with them, the energy they produce is easy to detect.

The easiest chakra to start with is the heart chakra. Hold one of your hands approximately twelve inches in front of your body. Your palm should face your chest. Slowly move your hand toward your chest until you feel a slight resistance. Once you feel it, draw your hand away until the resistance disappears, and then move it forward again until the resistance reoccurs. You are feeling your heart chakra.

Repeat this exercise, but this time place your hand a few inches away from your heart chakra. Slowly move your palm toward your body until you feel the now-familiar feeling of resistance. You'll notice that the resistance occurs much closer to your body than it did when you were feeling your heart chakra. This demonstrates the degree of energy produced by the chakras, and makes them easy to locate.

Once you've felt your heart chakra, you can use the same method to locate the other chakras. You will have to hold your hand over your head to locate your crown chakra.

While you have been doing these experiments, your partner will also have been doing them at his or her home. Now it's time to feel each other's auras.

FEELING OTHER PEOPLE'S AURAS

You and your friend should complete the solo exercises before starting to feel other people's auras.

Ask your friend to sit down comfortably on a straight-backed chair. Stand behind him or her and hold your hands about twelve inches away from either side of your friend's head. Gradually bring your hands closer until you feel a slight resistance. Test this by moving your hands slightly in different directions to confirm that you are in contact with your friend's aura. Frequently, your friend will feel a sensation in his or her aura at the moment you make contact with it.

Once you have confirmed that you are touching the aura, follow the aura with your hands along your friend's head, neck, and shoulders. Do this several times, and then swap places. If you like, you can do this experiment with your friend standing, and feel the aura all the way down to his or her feet.

You are likely to notice that the aura changes in different places. It may feel warmer, cooler, condensed, expanded, or even virtually undetectable at certain places. The aura may feel "sticky" in certain places. You may feel pins and needles in the palms of your hands as you move them over different parts of your friend's aura.

These marked changes in the aura are comparatively easy to detect, but it usually takes practice to recognize them instantly. In addition to them, you may sense slighter, more gradual changes as you move your hands around the aura. It is common, for instance, for the energy around the front of a person to feel noticeably different than the energy around the back. You're also likely to notice more energy around the person's head than the rest of the body.

You can also perform this exercise with family pets and plants, as their auras can also be felt and measured. We used to have a Siamese cat who loved having her aura stroked. We used to joke that she loved it even more than having her coat stroked.

The only problem people have with this exercise is that although they can feel something, they think they're imagining it. The remedy to this is to keep practicing. The more you do this, the more your confidence will increase, as will your sensitivity to auric energy.

HOW TO FEEL OTHER PEOPLE'S CHAKRAS

If you have been successful in the previous exercise, you will have no difficulty feeling your friend's chakras. This experiment should be done initially with only one layer of clothing. The less clothing your partner is wearing, the easier it is to feel the chakras. However, once you become more experienced, you'll be able to feel the chakras through several layers of clothing.

Ask your friend to lie down on a bed and close his or her eyes. Start feeling for the chakras in a random order. If you're doing it correctly, your friend will be able to tell you which chakra you are feeling.

Swap places after you've successfully found all seven of the main chakras. It's an interesting sensation to feel someone making contact with your chakras, and it also serves to remind you that you're both developing your skills at aura awareness.

SENSING THE PSYCHOLOGICAL AURA

Everyone has their own personal space, and most people feel uncomfortable when someone they don't know stands too close to them. People who live in the country usually have much larger personal spaces than people who live in cities. My father-in-law was a farmer, and he felt most comfortable when people stood several feet away from him. I often wondered how he'd fare in a crowded, rush-hour commuter train.

People from different countries have wide variations of personal space, too. People from Asian countries, for instance, have a smaller personal space than the average American. As a result, a visitor from the Far East could unintentionally cause an American to back across the room, as he would constantly, without realizing it, enter the American's personal space. Dr. Charles Tart, the American psychologist and parapsychologist, calls this personal space the "psychological aura."[2]

This experiment will help you detect the psychological aura. One person will need to stand facing the wall at one side of a room, with his or her arms and legs spread. The other person stands at the far end of the room, then proceeds to approach the other person as quietly as possible. The person facing the wall has to detect when his or her friend enters the psychological aura.

This experiment is not as easy as it sounds. During the first few attempts, the person facing the wall will be extremely aware that his or her friend is approaching, and may subconsciously feel that he or she is closer than is the case.

The other problem is that because the two of you are friends, your auras are likely to intermingle freely, so you may not sense the intrusion as much as you would if you were doing this experiment with a stranger.

Whenever I do this experiment, I focus on my breathing and try to ignore any sounds from inside or outside the room. By doing this, not always, but most of the time, it is obvious when the other person enters my psychological aura.

VISUALIZING THE AURA

This is an interesting experiment that often shows that people are subconsciously sensing the colors in people's auras before they can see them visually.

You'll need a large sheet of cream or white paper and some colored markers or pencils.

Ask your friend to stand several feet away from you with arms and legs uncrossed while facing you. Any light source should be behind you, and not be focused directly on your friend.

In the center of your sheet of paper, draw a rough outline of your friend's body. This is not a drawing exercise, and your outline should be as basic and simple as possible.

Draw a large oval around the outline, and then draw two slightly larger ones outside the first one.

Gaze at your friend while relaxing as much as possible. When you feel ready, use your intuition and pick up a marker or pencil. Use it to color in the first oval. Repeat with the other two ovals. It's possible to use the same marker or pencil more than once. Once you've colored in the ovals, you may, if you wish, pick up another pencil or marker and draw lines radiating out through the aura from the body.

The three ovals represent three layers of your friend's aura. The first layer represents the physical aspects of the person. The second is the emotional layer, and the third is the mental layer.

Once you have finished your aura drawing, swap places and allow your friend to draw his or her visualization of your aura.

Keep these pictures. Once you're able to see auras, it will be interesting to see how accurate you were with visualizing, rather than seeing, the aura. I believe many aura readers "see" auras through visualization, rather than through their eyes. In this book I'm able to teach you how I see auras, but my methods are just one of many techniques.

Do not rush through these experiments. You will make more progress with several short sessions than you will with one or two long ones. Make sure that you approach these experiments with a sense of playfulness and fun. Both you and your friend should have a good time, with plenty of laughter and jokes, while doing these initial exercises. A lighthearted, yet serious, approach will always produce better results than one done with grim determination.

Make sure to practice all of the experiments in this chapter before moving on to the next chapter. In chapter 3 we'll examine the different aspects of color and color symbolism, as well as the basic meanings of each color.

3

YOU ARE A RAINBOW

WE ARE ALL affected by color. It is, for instance, impossible to buy something that is not colored. We stop when traffic lights turn red, and start again when they change to green. The color choices we make in our own homes reflect our personalities. We may think we're using logic when it comes to making color choices. However, our initial response to color is always psychological because color affects us all at a deep subconscious level.

Some colors are cheerful and uplifting, while others make us feel flat and lacking in energy. Some colors stimulate and excite, while others depress and even antagonize. A brightly colored room raises our spirits. A room with violet walls calms us down. People who claim to be insensitive to color still notice their changes in mood, even if they are not consciously aware of the colors in the room. Even the colors of different foods stimulate our appetite. The colors of spring fill us with energy and zest for life while autumnal colors are more subdued and somber. Wearing certain colors gives us confidence, and can also affect the way people react to us.

Knowledge of this can be put to practical use. Violent prisoners, for instance, become calm and docile when placed in pink cells. A factory increased production by 8 percent merely by painting the walls of the bathrooms a "ghastly electric green," which discouraged people from staying in them for long.[1]

Almost everyone has a favorite color. This color is determined by a number of factors, including the person's age, gender, ethnicity, and income. Even climate plays a role in determining favorite colors. People who live in warm climates usually prefer strong, vibrant, and warm colors, while people who live in cooler climates prefer cooler colors. People's color preferences sometimes change, too, as they progress through life. This is determined largely by the person's age and improvement in socioeconomic status.

In the first chapter of Genesis, the first book of the Bible, "God said, Let there be light: and there was light." (Genesis 1:3) Light is essential for life, and color comes from light. There is no color in the absence of light. Light is made up of different wavelengths in the visible spectrum, as well as ultraviolet light that we cannot see. The longest wavelength, with the lowest frequency, is red. Violet has the shortest wavelength, and the highest frequency.

In 1665, the Black Death temporarily closed down Cambridge University. Consequently, a twenty-three-year-old graduate student named Isaac Newton (1642–1727), later to become a renowned physicist and mathematician, returned home with the intention of improving the telescope, which was the most advanced scientific instrument of his time. The problem with the existing telescopes was the lenses, and Isaac Newton ground new lenses that would enable all the light rays to focus at the same point. Unfortunately, the edges of his new lenses acted like prisms and created rims of color.

Isaac became fascinated with this anomaly and devised an experiment to examine each color in turn. He then turned his attention to the properties of a prism and discovered that all the colors of the rainbow—red, orange, yellow, green, blue, indigo, and violet—are contained in white light. He did this by using a prism to create a spectrum of color, and then used a second prism to convert the spectrum back to a beam of light. This was a revolutionary discovery at the time, as until then, everyone believed color was a solid, integral part of every object.

Rainbows are created by droplets of water in the atmosphere acting as prisms that refract and reflect the rays of the sun. From the time of Aristotle, people had tried to find out what caused the vivid bands of color that create a rainbow. The fact that they could appear almost anywhere, and always had the same arrangement of colors, must have been an incredible mystery that remained unsolved until the young Isaac Newton experimented with prisms.

Light and color enable us to see part of the electromagnetic spectrum. In fact, visible light represents only one-sixtieth of the electromagnetic spectrum.

Many animals experience color differently than humans. Bees, for instance, are sensitive to ultraviolet light, which is beyond the range of our eyes. This ability to see ultraviolet may help bees find pollen in flowers. Birds can also see ultraviolet light. In addition, they have four types of cones in their retinas, which enable them to see a wider range of colors than we do. (Humans have three types of cones.)

Cats, foxes, and owls can see much better at night than we can because they can see longer wavelengths of light. This includes infrared waves that we experience only as heat. If you've ever wondered how cats can always find the warmest place in the house, it's because they can "see" heat. However, your cat can't see the full range of colors that we do.

Red has a particular frequency and wavelength, as do all the other colors. A wall that is painted red will absorb all the wavelengths of visible light except for red. Likewise, a blue object will absorb all the wavelengths except for blue. A black object will absorb every color, while something that is white will reflect all the colors of visible white light.

Our eyes distinguish color using the retina at the back of the eye. When light rays enter the eye, the lens focuses them on the rods and cones in the retina. The rods are sensitive to light, but largely ignore color. The rods enable us to discern what is going on in poor light. There are three types of cones that contain pigments that absorb the different wavelengths of light. Some of the cones recognize and absorb long wavelengths (red, orange, and yellow). Others absorb the middle (green) and short (blue, indigo, and violet) wavelengths. As the light reaches the various cones, the pigment sends a message through the optic nerve to the brain, which interprets the message, enabling us to see color.

SYNESTHESIA

A few people are able to "see" tastes and scents as colors. Although many people can imagine a color relating to a particular taste or smell, synesthetics do more than this, as they actually experience seeing the colors. There are different types of synesthesia. Some people experience sounds as colors, and vice versa, while others relate letters and certain words to different colors.

Franz Liszt, the composer and pianist, had synesthesia, as did Vladimir Nabakov, the author, and David Hockney, the artist.

Edvard Munch (1863–1944), the Norwegian artist, painted *The Scream*, his most famous painting, in 1893. One evening, feeling tired and unwell, Edvard Munch watched the sun set over a fjord. He wrote: "I was tired and ill—I stood looking out across the fjord—the sun was setting—the clouds were coloured red—like blood—I felt as though a scream went through nature—I thought I heard a scream—I painted this picture—painted the clouds like real blood—the colours were screaming."[2] This is a rare example of someone hearing sounds from colors. Usually, it occurs the other way around.

Today, people study color for many reasons. Because different colors affect us emotionally, marketers continually experiment with them to sell more products.

COLOR SENSING

Some blind people are able to sense colors by holding their hands over objects of different colors. They can feel the different wavelengths of light on their skin, and recognize which colors feel "hot" or "cold."

In my psychic development classes, I found that many people have the potential to develop this skill. All you need are swatches of material or paper in a variety of different colors. Close your eyes, and ask someone to mix the swatches and place them in a row in front of you. Using either your palms or fingertips, see if you can sense the various colors as you move your hands over the line of samples.

Everyone is different. Some people find this a comparatively easy test, but most people have to persevere for days, or even weeks, before achieving success. In my experience, some people are unable to develop this skill. If at first you find it impossible to do, forget about it for a month or two, and then try again. Remember that the best results come when you approach the experiment in a spirit of fun.

COLOR SYMBOLISM

Colors have strong symbolic associations that sometimes date back thousands of years. Most color symbolism comes from nature. Green, for instance, symbolizes nature, and gold symbolizes the sun. Blue symbolizes the sky, but also spirituality as heaven is thought to be in the sky.

Red

As red is the color of blood, it symbolizes life itself. Red is active and symbolizes energy, aggression, war, fire, emotions, passion, joy, vitality, and strength. Because of this, red also has sexual connotations. Prostitutes advertise their services with a red light, and "scarlet" women are said to be promiscuous. Red can also symbolize anger and rage, as the phrase "seeing red" indicates.

In ancient Egypt, red and orange symbolized the sun god, Ra. In Buddhism, red is the color of creativity and life. In Christianity, red is a sacrificial color, symbolizing Christ's passion.

Orange

Orange symbolizes fertility, love, luxury, and comfort. In China and Japan, orange symbolizes love and happiness. Oranges are eaten on the second day of the Chinese New Year to attract good luck in the coming year.

Yellow

Yellow symbolizes sunlight, strength, laughter, and the joys of life. St. Peter is often depicted wearing yellow robes. However, there is another side to yellow. It has long been associated with cowardice and betrayal. This is why Judas Iscariot is often shown wearing yellow robes, and cowards are said to be "yellow."

Yellow is a sacred color in Buddhism, and their monks wear saffron robes. Gautama Buddha deliberately chose the color yellow, which had previously been worn by criminals, to symbolize his humility and detachment from the materialistic world. In Hinduism, yellow symbolizes light, truth, and immortality.

Green

Green symbolizes balance and healing. Around the world it symbolizes fertility, rebirth, renewal, spring, youth, and growth.

Green is a sacred color in Islam. This is because the Prophet is never depicted as a person, but is believed to be present in every part of nature.

Blue

Blue symbolizes love, sincerity, faith, honesty, and hope. It also relates to purity, eternity, devotion, chastity, and spirituality.

Because of its close connection with spirituality, many sky gods were associated with the color blue. These include, the Egyptian Amun, the Greek Zeus, the Roman Jupiter, and the Hindu gods Indra, Vishnu, and Krishna (who also had blue skin). In Christian art, the Virgin Mary is usually shown wearing blue. In Buddhism, blue symbolizes wisdom and the peace and calm of the heavens. In the Hebrew tradition, blue symbolizes mercy.

Purple

Purple symbolizes intuition and the imagination. The ancient Romans associated it with dignity and power as purple was worn by high priests, magistrates, and military leaders. A son born to a reigning sovereign is said to be "born to the purple." When a priest becomes a cardinal, he is "raised to the purple."

In Christianity, purple symbolizes the mystery of the Lord's passion, which is why it is used during Lent.

White

White is the color of purity, truth, innocence, and virginity, which explains why many brides choose a white wedding dress. White is also the color of initiation. The word "candidate" comes from the Latin word for "shining white."

White has been considered a spiritual color since the founding of the Zoroastrian religion in the sixth century BCE. In Christian art, Jesus wore white robes after his resurrection. A white dove symbolizes peace and the Holy Spirit.

Black

Black has always had negative connotations. It symbolizes death, sorrow, despair, and mourning. It is also related to evil and the "dark arts."

In ancient Egypt, black had more positive symbolism. Black cats were sacred. Anubis, who led souls to the afterlife, was black. Dark earth and black clouds symbolized germination, which takes place in the dark.

COLOR VISUALIZATION

Color visualization can be used in many ways. If someone or something has made you angry, you can release the negativity with a color visualization. You can release long-held negative emotions in the same way. You can use it for positive purposes, too, such as gaining confidence, courage, and motivation. It can be used for protection purposes, and to help develop athletic and sporting ability. You can also use visualization to enhance your color awareness.

Enhancing Color Awareness Visualization

In this visualization you'll walk through a rainbow, pausing in each color to experience the effects each color has on you. I usually prefer to do these visualizations on my own, but you can, if you wish, ask your partner to guide you through the visualization.

You will need to set aside about thirty minutes to complete this exercise. I like to perform it while sitting comfortably in a reclining chair or lying down on the floor. If I do this exercise in bed I'm inclined to fall asleep halfway through the rainbow. Make sure the room is pleasantly warm, and that you are wearing loose-fitting clothes. You might want to cover yourself with a blanket.

Take three slow, deep breaths, and then relax all the muscles in your body, starting with your toes and feet and working your way up your body to the top of your head. Once you have done this, mentally scan your body to see if any area is still tense. If so, focus on it until it relaxes.

When you feel totally relaxed, imagine yourself in a beautiful landscape. This may be a scene you remember from the past, or it might be a pleasant environment you create in your mind. Visualize yourself walking through this beautiful landscape.

Ahead of you is the start of a beautiful rainbow that reaches far up into the sky. You are surprised and delighted that you're so close to the start of a rainbow, and you walk a little faster to see if you can reach it.

Much to your amazement, you suddenly see yourself at the foot of the rainbow. You pause, and gaze at it with mounting excitement. From where you are standing, you can see all the colors of the rainbow. They seem so much more vibrant now that you're standing right beside them. You decide to walk into the rainbow, starting with the color red.

You feel a slight resistance as you enter the rainbow, but suddenly you're inside and completely surrounded by the color red. It is the most gorgeous red you have ever seen, and you take big breaths of red energy deep into your lungs. The red invigorates and empowers you, filling you with confidence and energy. You feel as if you could do anything you set your mind on. You walk deeper into the red, feeling more and more powerful with each step. You know now, with every fiber of your being, that you are far more capable than you had previously imagined.

As you walk, the red gradually turns to orange, and you feel surrounded with harmony and love. You feel a strong desire to forgive everyone who has ever harmed you, and to forgive yourself for any harm you may have caused others. You sense that the orange is revitalizing every cell in your body. You feel more at peace than you've ever felt before.

Enjoy the feelings of orange for as long as you wish, and then walk into the yellow. You immediately sense the mental stimulation yellow gives you. You suddenly feel mentally energized and full of ideas about your life and the future you want.

Again, when you feel ready, move on into the green. As you gaze at the beautiful green that surrounds you, you feel a sense of peace and calm. It seems nothing could bother or disturb your feelings of tranquility and contentment. You can't remember when you felt so relaxed and contented.

It's tempting to remain in the green indefinitely, but eventually you start moving forward again and walk into the blue. You immediately sense feelings of freedom. The blue is clearer than any sky you've ever seen, and you feel a sense of excitement and adventure. You sense opportunities waiting for you in the near future, and you can't wait to get started on them.

You move into the indigo. You feel a sense of warmth, as if something was nurturing and encouraging you. You gaze into the indigo and feel a strong desire to help others, to enable them to experience the same opportunities that you have had.

After filling yourself with indigo energy, you move into the violet. As you do, you sense an awareness of the spiritual side of life, and realize that everyone is interconnected at the spiritual level. For a moment you feel the presence of the Divine in every cell of your body and understand the precious gift of life that has been freely given to you. The joy and happiness inside you builds and grows until you feel you can take no more.

Finally, you walk out the other side of the rainbow and lie down on the soft grass. When you feel ready to return to your everyday life, you take three deep breaths, open your eyes, stretch, and spend a minute or two thinking about the visualization before getting up.

This visualization is extremely useful in helping you gain awareness and understanding of each color of the rainbow. Once you know what feelings you experience with each color, you will be able to use the colors individually to help you in everyday life.

If you need additional confidence, for instance, all you need do is close your eyes for a few seconds and imagine yourself surrounded by pure red energy. Take some big gulps of the red air and open your eyes. You will find you have all the confidence you need to handle the situation. A friend of mine always visualizes himself surrounded by violet energy before saying his prayers. This immediately gets him in the right state of mind, and he feels his prayers are more effective as a result.

Emotional Release Visualization

Everyone experiences negative emotions. For most people, they occur every now and again, and quickly disappear. Some people, though, become totally consumed with negative thoughts and feelings. This visualization is designed to help you release any negativity in your life.

Start in the same way as the previous visualization by making yourself comfortable and relaxing as much as possible. When you feel totally relaxed, let your mind think about your problems and concerns. Notice any sensations in your body as you do this. You may feel a tightening in your stomach, or a constriction in your breathing.

Think of your main concern, and try to look at it as if you were an observer, rather than the person who is experiencing it. In your mind, give your negative emotion a shape, color, and size. Feel the shape and see if it feels hard or soft, cool or warm, wet or dry. Allow the shape to grow larger, and then smaller. Notice if the emotion intensifies when you allow the shape to grow, and reduces when the shape becomes smaller.

If you wish, you can question the shape and see what replies come into your mind. When you have received all the information you need, reduce the size of the shape until it is almost invisible. Take three slow deep breaths, and open your eyes.

Spend a minute or two thinking about the experience you have just had before getting up. If reducing the size of your problem to an insignificant level seems to have released it, you can continue with your day. However, if you can still feel the emotion, you can take one more step.

You'll need colored pencils or markers and a sheet of paper. Draw the image of your negative emotion. Put all your anger, pain, and suffering into the drawing. It doesn't matter if you have no artistic ability. No one needs to see what you've produced, and you'll find it highly therapeutic to release your emotions in this manner.

Once you've completed your drawing, put it aside for an hour or two. If possible, leave it overnight and look at it again on the following day.

When you examine it again, notice the colors you chose. If you were angry, you might have chosen red as your main color. Red can represent rage, fury, and anger. However, it can also symbolize power and energy. It all depends how it is used.

Look at the shape and size of your emotion. Notice how much pressure you used when drawing it. Pause, and see how your body feels when you look at the drawing.

Repeat the visualization, followed by the drawing, and continue doing this every day until you can look at the most recent drawing without feeling any emotion at all in your body.

A friend of mine does this exercise in a slightly different way. He draws the emotion in the usual way, but when he looks at his drawing again the next day, he deliberately redraws it using bright, cheerful colors. He also makes the shape smoother and more rounded. He says this reduces the ability of the emotion to have any affect upon him.

COLOR IN THE AURA

The colors of your aura are vibrant, intense, luminous vibrations of energy created by the electromagnetic charge of your aura. This frequency level is slightly beyond the range of light that the average human eye can see, but it can be photographed, and almost everyone can learn to see it, if they're prepared to work at it. We'll cover how to see the aura in chapter 5.

The colors inside the aura swirl, intermingle, and change depending on the person's thoughts, feelings, health, and energy. However, the main colors in the aura remain constant and provide clues as to the person's ability and purpose in life.

Inside the aura are seven powerful conductors of energy called the chakras. You'll learn how to sense and work with these in the next chapter.

4

THE CHAKRAS

THE WORD *CHAKRA* is the Sanskrit word for "wheel." In the East, the chakras are often depicted as lotus flowers, each one with a different number of petals. Chakras are revolving, wheel-like circles of subtle energy that absorb higher energies, including the universal life force, and transform them into a useable form that the body can utilize. They play a major role in the person's physical, mental, and emotional health, and act as powerful batteries that energize the entire body. Although the chakras are non-physical, they have a powerful effect on how we function physically.

The concept of chakras dates back thousands of years, and much of what we know about them can be found in the Hindu *Upanishads* (c.900–400 BCE). Although the chakras have been utilized in the East for thousands of years, it was not until the 1970s that scientists in the West began investigating them.

One of the most important scientists was Dr. Horoshi Motoyama, who conducted experiments intended to prove or disprove the existence of chakras. His tests, conducted inside a specially designed lead-lined booth, were intended to measure the bioenergetic/bioelectrical output from the chakras. Moveable copper electrodes were placed close to the chakras being tested to measure the bioelectrical field. Dr. Motoyama discovered that the amplitude and frequency of the electrical field around the chakra was significantly greater in people who claimed they had awakened or opened specific chakras than it was in his test subjects. Dr. Motoyama also discovered that some people could create electrical field disturbances by deliberately projecting energy through their chakras. This experiment has been successfully demonstrated on many occasions at different university laboratories around the world.[1] Dr. Motoyama published his findings in his book, *Science and the Evolution of Consciousness: Chakras, Ki, and Psi*.[2]

In the late 1970s, Dr. Valerie Hunt conducted a series of experiments involving auras and the chakras at UCLA. One experiment, using EMG (electromyography) electrodes, was conducted to determine the therapeutic effects of a manipulative technique known as Rolfing. She discovered that the readings the electrodes measured over the chakra positions were significantly higher than in other parts of the body.[3]

Hindu yogis believe that *prana* (the life force) travels through the body using a network of tiny channels called *nadis*. There are said to be 72,000 nadis inside the human aura.[4] The main nadi, known as the *sushumna*, runs along the length of the spine and connects the seven most important chakras. On either side of the sushumna are two other nadis, known as *ida* (on the left) and *pingala* (on the right). Ida carries purifying lunar energy, while pingala carries solar energy. In most traditions, these three nadi run parallel to each other, but in some traditions they interweave between the different chakras and meet at the crown chakra.

The human body contains currents of both positive and negative energies that influence the directions the chakras revolve in. The right side of the body contains positive energy, and the left side negative. The chakras appear to revolve in the opposite direction to the chakras immediately above and below them.

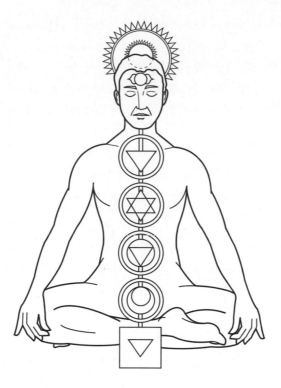

The seven main chakras are situated at different places alongside the spine, and act as powerful batteries or energy centers that stimulate the physical and subtle bodies they connect and look after. Each chakra is related to a physical system and the organs associated with it. For instance, the root chakra influences the large intestine and the rectum. The sacral chakra influences the kidneys, bladder, and reproductive systems. The solar, or solar plexus, chakra influences the liver, gall bladder, stomach, spleen, and small intestine. The heart chakra influences the heart and the arms. The throat chakra influences the throat and lungs. The brow chakra influences the brain, and the crown chakra plays an important role in looking after the entire being.

There is an immediate and direct relationship between the state of each chakra and the health of the organs it is connected to. Chakras can be open, closed, blocked, and both in and out of balance. Any changes made to the chakras to restore them to balance will have an effect on the physical body.

It is rare to find someone with every chakra open and in balance. This person would feel fulfilled, joyful, and contented. Most people experience fluctuations in the state of individual chakras caused by fear, stress, and frustration.

THE QUATERN

The chakras are often represented as a square and a triangle. The four bottom chakras represent the square and are known as the quatern. These chakras have a slower vibration than the three uppermost chakras. Each of them represents one of the traditional elements of earth, water, fire, and air. It is important to remember that even though the four chakras in the quatern are lower than the three in the trinity, all seven chakras are equal in value to each other. They all have their own specific purposes and are equally important.

Root Chakra (Muladhara)

COLOR: Red

ELEMENT: Earth

FUNCTION: Survival

GLANDS: Adrenals

PETALS: Four

SENSE: Smell

DESIRES: Physical contact

CHALLENGE: To think before acting

KEYWORD: Physical

The Sanskrit word for the root chakra is *muladhara*, which comes from *mula* meaning "root," and *adhara*, "support." It is often called the "base" or "support" chakra. This chakra is situated at the base of the spine in the area of the coccyx, and keeps us firmly grounded to the earth. It is concerned with self-preservation and provides feelings of security and comfort. It gives us vitality, energy, and a sense of really being alive. At its most basic, it symbolizes survival and the life force. At an emotional level it gives us courage, strength, and persistence. The root chakra plays a major role in our survival as it controls our fight-or-flight responses. This chakra also governs our sense of smell and the solid parts of our body, such as teeth, bones, and nails. Unlike the other chakras, the root chakra faces downward toward the earth.

When the root chakra is understimulated, the person will feel nervous and insecure. Consequently, digestive problems and fear can gather inside this chakra. When the root chakra is overstimulated, the person will be domineering, self-centered, and addicted to money, power, and sex.

Sacral Chakra (Svadisthana)

COLOR: Orange

ELEMENT: Water

FUNCTION: Sexuality, creativity, pleasure

GLANDS: Ovaries, testicles

PETALS: Six

SENSE: Taste

DESIRES: Respect and acceptance

CHALLENGE: To love and serve others

KEYWORD: Social

The sacral chakra is situated at the level of the sacrum in the lower abdomen, approximately two inches below the navel. As this chakra is related to the element of water, it is concerned with the fluidic functions of the body. It represents creativity, emotional balance and sexuality. The Sanskrit word *svadisthana* means "home of the vital force." The sacral chakra stimulates hope and optimism at an emotional level. It also relates to the sense of taste. People who relate well to others have well-balanced sacral chakras, as it gives them the necessary fluidity to interact with others easily. When this chakra is blocked, or not working as well as it should, the person is likely to experience arthritis, urinary problems, or sexual dysfunction, along with a loss of personal power. These difficulties are frequently caused by the negative emotions of anger, frustration, and resentment that are created when this chakra is understimulated. If this chakra is overstimulated the person will be aggressive, manipulative, and overly self-indulgent.

Solar Plexus Chakra (Manipura)

COLOR: Yellow

ELEMENT: Fire

FUNCTION: Will, personal power

GLANDS: Pancreas

PETALS: Ten

SENSE: Sight

DESIRES: To understand

CHALLENGE: To communicate effectively with loved ones

KEYWORD: Intellect

The word *manipura* means "jewel of the navel." The solar plexus chakra is situated between the navel and the sternum. This chakra provides us with personal power, warmth, confidence, healthy self-esteem, and happiness. When it's working efficiently, it relates to the absorption and assimilation of food, and provides good digestion and a feeling of physical well-being.

This chakra also relates to the eyes, which is not surprising, as everything seems brighter when we feel contented and happy. The solar plexus chakra also relates to sensitivity and the emotions. It enhances creativity, optimism, trust, confidence, and self-respect at an emotional level. However, it also enhances anger and hostility when the person has a negative approach to life. If the chakra is overstimulated, the person will be an overly demanding, perfectionist workaholic. If it is understimulated, the person will lack confidence, be overly sensitive to the reactions of others, and feel that he or she has little or no control over circumstances and events. This can create ulcers and stomach disorders.

Heart Chakra (Anahatha)

COLOR: Green

ELEMENT: Air

FUNCTION: Love

GLANDS: Thymus

PETALS: Twelve

SENSE: Touch

DESIRES: To love and be loved

CHALLENGE: To gain confidence

KEYWORD: Emotions

The heart chakra is situated in the center of the chest, in line with the heart. The word *anahatha* means "unstruck" or "unbeaten." This relates to an eternal sound or note that can be heard, even though it has not been created by any human instrument. The heart chakra relates to personal and unconditional love, harmony, sympathetic understanding, healing, and the sense of touch. This is because when we are "in touch" with someone our heart (emotions) goes out to him or her. On an emotional level, the heart chakra enhances compassion, self-acceptance, and respect for self and others. People with well-balanced heart chakras are in touch with their feelings and nurture themselves and encourage others. If the heart chakra is understimulated the person will be overly sensitive, overly sympathetic, and have a need to give to others. This person will feel afraid and sorry for himself or herself. Most codependants have an understimulated heart chakra. If this chakra is overstimulated, the person will be possessive, controlling, demanding, and moody.

THE TRINITY

The three uppermost chakras are known as the trinity or triad. They vibrate at a higher level than the four chakras of the quatern. The three chakras of the trinity relate to the quadruplicities of astrology known as cardinal, fixed, and mutable. The cardinal signs (Aries, Cancer, Libra, and Capricorn) are outgoing, energetic, and expressive. The fixed signs (Taurus, Leo, Scorpio, and Aquarius) are rigid, stubborn, and tenacious. The mutable signs (Gemini, Virgo, Sagittarius, and Pisces) are adaptable and able to adjust to changing circumstances.

Highly evolved people have active brow and crown chakras. Unfortunately, few people expend energy in developing these chakras and work mainly with the lower five chakras. Many years ago, Alice A. Bailey made a profound comment on the current state of human evolution when she wrote: "The throat center is beginning to make itself felt with the head [brow and crown] and heart centers still asleep."[5]

Throat Chakra (Visshudha)

COLOR: Blue

QUADRUPLICITY: Fixed

FUNCTION: Communication, creativity

GLANDS: Thyroid and parathyroid

PETALS: Sixteen

SENSE: Sound

DESIRES: Inner peace

CHALLENGE: To risk

KEYWORD: Concepts

The throat chakra is situated at the level of the throat. The word *visshudha* means "pure." The throat chakra is the chakra of communication and self-expression, especially when spoken. It seeks the truth in all things. It plays a vital role in transmitting thoughts and ideas from the brow chakra to the four lower chakras. At an emotional level, the throat chakra enhances idealism, love, and understanding. When it is balanced, this chakra provides contentment, peace of mind, a good sense of timing, and a strong faith. Someone with a blanced throat chakra will be kind and considerate of others. When this chakra is overstimulated, the person will be arrogant, dogmatic, overbearing, and sarcastic. He or she will speak at great length, but be unwilling to listen to others. When it is understimulated, the person will be uncommunicative, weak, fearful, devious, and unreliable. This person may well experience problems with his or her neck and shoulders.

Brow Chakra (Ajna)

COLOR: Indigo

QUADRUPLICITY: Mutable

FUNCTION: Intuition, thought, perception

GLANDS: Pituitary

PETALS: Ninety-six

DESIRES: To be in harmony with the universe

CHALLENGE: To turn one's dreams into reality

KEYWORD: Intuition

The brow chakra is situated in the forehead, just above the eyebrows. The Sanskrit word *ajna* means "command." This is a good name, as the brow chakra governs the mind and controls all the other chakras. At an emotional level, this chakra increases our understanding of the everyday world by making us aware of our spiritual natures. We pick up other people's thoughts, feelings, and even intuitions with the brow chakra. The brow chakra is frequently referred to as "the third eye," as it is concerned with psychic and spiritual matters. When this chakra is overstimulated, the person will be proud, authoritative, manipulative, and dogmatic. When it is understimulated, the person will be timid, hesitant, non-assertive, and prone to tension headaches.

Crown Chakra (Sahasrara)

COLOR: Violet

QUADRUPLICITY: Cardinal

FUNCTION: Union with the Divine

GLANDS: Pineal

PETALS: Nine-hundred-and-seventy-two

DESIRES: Universal understanding

CHALLENGE: To grow in knowledge and wisdom

KEYWORD: Spirituality

The crown chakra is situated at the top of the head and is often depicted as a halo when artists paint someone who is spiritually evolved. The Sanskrit word *sahasrara* means "thousand," and the symbol of the crown chakra is the thousand-petaled lotus.

The crown chakra balances and harmonizes the often-conflicting sides of our natures. It also governs the mystical and spiritual level that enables us to gain insight and understand the interconnectedness of all living things. It cannot be activated until all the other chakras have been mastered and are in a state of balance. When it is balanced, this chakra brings enlightenment and a sense of being at one with the entire universe. When the crown chakra is overstimulated, the person will be frustrated, depressed, and destructive. This person is also likely to suffer from severe migraine headaches. When the crown chakra is understimulated, the person will be withdrawn, taciturn, and unable to experience any of the joys of life.

CHAKRA MANTRAS

The first six chakras have sounds, known as bija mantras, assigned to them. *Bija* means "seed," and is the root sound of each chakra. A mantra is a word or phrase that is repeated over and over again to induce a relaxed, meditative state. The bija mantras can be chanted, or silently vibrated, to stimulate and open up the chakras. They can also help you feel the chakras, as you will sense the vibration in your body as you repeat the mantra.

The mantras are:

ROOT CHAKRA: Lam (pronounced lum)

SACRAL CHAKRA: Vam (pronounced vum)

SOLAR PLEXUS CHAKRA: Ram (pronounced rum)

HEART CHAKRA: Yam (pronounced yum)

THROAT CHAKRA: Ham (pronounced hum)

BROW CHAKRA: Om (pronounced or-mmmm)

To experiment with these, sit or lie down comfortably. Close your eyes, and take several slow deep breaths. When you feel relaxed, say the first mantra (lam) out loud each time you exhale. Repeat this for about five minutes, and be alert to any feelings you experience in the area of your root chakra. You may feel a sense of warmth, or the opposite, a feeling of coolness. You may experience a tickling or prickly sensation. You may not feel anything, but experience an awareness of your root chakra. Everyone is different, and the response you receive as a result of performing this exercise will be the correct response for you. It's possible that you won't experience anything the first few times you practice this. That doesn't matter, as you will ultimately receive a response if you keep practicing. Don't spend longer than five minutes at a time on this exercise. If nothing happens in five minutes, it is better to forget about the exercise temporarily, rather than continue indefinitely and get frustrated.

Once you're able to awaken the root chakra with its mantra, you can move on to the sacral chakra. In time, and with practice, you will be able to awaken all six chakras using their mantras. The crown chakra will also awaken as a result of this, once the other six have been activated in this way.

When you're ready to finish the meditation, stop saying the mantra and focus on your breathing again. Take several slow, deep breaths, become aware of your surroundings, and open your eyes.

EXPERIENCING THE CHAKRAS

This is a fascinating visualization exercise that enables you to experience the energy of the chakras. It also makes it possible for you to ask any questions you may have about individual chakras.

1. Lie down and relax your body as much as possible.

2. Focus your attention on your root chakra, and visualize it as clearly as possible. Take three slow, deep breaths and imagine you're sending red energy to stimulate your root chakra. As you do this, imagine your root chakra responding to this attention in a positive way. (As the root chakra is always open, it's not necessary to open it.)

3. Shift your attention to the area of your sacral chakra, and again visualize it as clearly as you can. Take three slow, deep breaths and imagine you're sending orange energy into this chakra. Visualize it opening up like a blossom.

4. Repeat with your solar plexus, heart, throat, brow, and crown chakras, sending them the color that relates to them.

5. Decide on a chakra you'd like to explore further. You may have a specific reason for this, or you may simply choose a chakra by chance.

6. Focus on this chakra and, in your imagination, allow yourself to walk into a room that represents this chakra. Pay attention to how it feels inside this room, and what effect, if any, this has on your physical body. Notice the color scheme and how the room is furnished. Walk around and explore the room. Pause and look at any pictures there may be on the walls.

7. When you have finished your exploration of the room, walk into the center of the room and sit down in one of two comfortable chairs that are there. Ask the guardian of the room to join you. Visualize this person coming into the room and sitting down in the other chair.

8. Spend a few minutes asking the guardian of the room any questions you have about this particular chakra. You may have specific questions that relate to you or people close to you. You may have more general questions about the chakra and how it works.

9. Once you have finished your conversation, thank the guardian of the room and say goodbye.

10. In your imagination, return to your brow chakra and visualize the petals closing down gently. Repeat with the throat, heart, solar plexus, and sacral chakras. The crown and root chakras are not included as they are always kept open.

11. Take a few slow, deep breaths, allow yourself to return to the room you are performing the exercise in, and when you feel ready, open your eyes.

12. Lie quietly for a minute or two before getting up.

I like to eat or drink something after this exercise, as it helps to ground me again. Once the exercise is over, think about the experience. Think about the room, and everything that was in it. Everything in that room has some meaning to you. I always pay particular attention to any paintings on the wall, as they usually relate to something that is going on in my life.

Repeat this exercise frequently. You can visit a different chakra each time, or you may prefer to visit the same chakra a number of times before moving on to explore another chakra.

I always feel peaceful and calm after performing this exercise.

CHAKRA BALANCING

The pendulum is a useful tool for discovering areas of negativity in the chakras. Everyone harbors negative thoughts and feelings at times, and a chakra balancing can release this negativity, providing the person with an immediate sense of happiness and well-being. Sometimes, if the negativity is longstanding, the person can look years younger after his or her chakras have been balanced.

A pendulum is a small weight attached to a thread, chain, or cord. It is used to read energy patterns and to learn information from our subconscious minds. Pendulums can be bought from New Age stores, or you may choose to make your own. My mother always used her wedding ring attached to a length of thread. The best pendulum for you is one that looks attractive and is comfortable to hold and use. Ideally, the pendulum should weigh about three ounces, be round, spherical, or cylindrical in shape, and preferably have a point at the bottom.

While looking for a suitable pendulum, you will probably see aura, or spectrum, pendulums. These pendulums have all the colors of the rainbow depicted on the side. They also have a small indicator that can be moved up and down to indicate the color you are dowsing for. This type of pendulum is useful for chakra balancing, but is not essential. I have one of these that I use for chakra balancing, but at least half the time I use one of my other pendulums.

Although you will be able to use a pendulum in a matter of minutes, it takes time to become proficient with it. Most people hold the pendulum with the hand they write with.

Sit down, rest your elbow on a table, and hold the thread or chain of your pendulum lightly between your thumb and index finger. Make sure that your elbow is the only part of your body that is in contact with the table. Make sure that your stomach, or any other part of your body, is not inadvertently touching the table. The palm of the hand holding the pendulum should be facing down, and the pendulum should be hanging freely about a foot in front of you.

Make sure that your hands and legs are uncrossed. Crossing your arms and hands subconsciously protects yourself, but also closes off the pendulum. You will be able to prove this to yourself once you have become familiar with your pendulum.

Swing the pendulum gently from side to side to become familiar with its movement. Allow it to swing in different directions. Deliberately swing the pendulum in circles. You might like to experiment with this while holding the thread at different lengths to see if the pendulum moves more readily for you when held at a certain position. Most people find the best result occurs when the thread is between four and five inches long. Experiment though, as you may find that a shorter or longer length works better for you. Everyone is different. Once you determine the best length, tie a knot, or mark the chain or thread, so you'll always know where to hold it for it to be at the optimum length.

Once you've become used to the movements of the pendulum, stop its movements with your free hand. When the pendulum is still, ask it which movement indicates a positive, or "yes," response. You can ask this question silently or out loud. Many people find that the pendulum will immediately move to indicate the positive direction. However, if this is your first time with a pendulum, it might take time before it moves. Be patient. It will probably make a slight movement to begin with, but if you keep thinking "yes," it will start moving more and more strongly.

There are four possible movements your pendulum can make. It might move toward and away from you, from side to side in front of you, or move in a clockwise or counterclockwise circle.

If you experience difficulty, gaze at the weight and imagine it moving to and fro. This normally encourages the pendulum to move. Allow it to move to and fro for about a minute, then stop it with your free hand and again ask it to indicate a positive response. If the pendulum does not move after about five minutes, put it away for a half hour, or even overnight, and try again. I have yet to meet anyone who is unable to use a pendulum. People who are open, imaginative, and willing to suspend belief usually find it easy to operate a pendulum, but with practice, anyone can succeed. Once you become used to the pendulum, the movements will occur almost as soon as you suspend your pendulum.

Once your pendulum has indicated a positive response, you can ask it to indicate the negative, or "no" direction. Follow this by asking your pendulum to indicate, "I don't know," and "I don't want to answer."

The four responses you receive will probably stay the same for the rest of your life. However, it still pays to check them every now and again, as I've met several people who have experienced changes in their pendulums' responses. The best time to check is when you have not used your pendulum for a while.

Once your pendulum is moving in response to your silent or spoken questions, you need to practice. Start by asking it questions that you already know the answers to. You might ask, "Am I female?" If you are, the pendulum should make a positive response. Obviously, it should give a negative response if you're male. You can ask similar questions about your name, marital status, number of children, and so on. After this, you should ask your pendulum questions for which you are seeking answers. The pendulum will be able to tap into your subconscious mind to find the answer, and then deliver it to your conscious mind by making the relevant movement that correctly answers your question.

There is one proviso with this, though. You have the ability to override the movements of the pendulum with your thoughts. Let's assume that you're asking for the sex of an unborn child. If you secretly hope that it will be a girl, for instance, the pendulum will reflect your innermost desires and confirm this, even though that may not be correct. If you have an emotional involvement in the answer to any question, you should ask someone who has no interest in the outcome to hold your pendulum for you.

The pendulum is a serious tool that should be used responsibly. If you ask it serious questions, you will always receive honest and correct answers. However, if you ask flippant questions, you'll receive the answers you deserve.

Once you've become familiar with your pendulum, you'll be able to use it for chakra balancing. Ask your friend to lie down comfortably on his or her back. Suspend your pendulum over his or her root chakra (the genital area), and ask your pendulum: "Is my friend's root chakra in good health?" (If you are using an aura pendulum, you should set the indicator to red before asking this question. You will need to change the indicator to orange when dowsing the sacral chakra, and continue changing it to indicate the color of each chakra in turn.) The pendulum will give either a positive or negative reply. If the answer is positive, nothing further needs to be done to this chakra, and you can move on to check the sacral chakra. If the answer is negative, more work will be required. Make a mental note of this and move on to the sacral chakra. Check all the chakras in the same way.

The next step is to determine which chakra is the most negative. You do this by suspending the pendulum over each of the chakras that gave a negative response in turn, and asking: "Is the (whatever it happens to be) chakra the most negative?" Continue asking questions of the negative chakras to establish their order of negativity.

Before proceeding further, you need to ask your pendulum two more questions: "Which movement indicates negative energies?" and "Which movement indicates positive energies?"

Fill a glass of water and place into it the fingers of the hand that does not hold the pendulum. Suspend the pendulum over the chakra that is the most negative and ask the pendulum to remove all the negative energies from it. Your pendulum will start moving in the direction that indicates negative energies. This shows that the pendulum is removing the negativity from the afflicted chakra. Visualize the negativity coming up the pendulum, into your arm, across your chest, and down into the glass of water.

When the pendulum stops moving in the negative direction, take your fingers out of the water and wash both hands thoroughly under running water. Empty the glass of water, and wash it thoroughly before filling it up again.

Repeat the process with the second most afflicted chakra, and continue the process until all the negative chakras have been treated.

Once you have done all of this, go through all seven chakras again to confirm that all the negativity has been removed and the chakras are now in balance. Sometimes you'll find that not all of the negativity has been removed, and you'll need to repeat the process of removing it. The chakras are not in balance until you receive a positive reading from each chakra.

The final step of the process is to visualize the color green and deliberately swing the pendulum all over the person's body in the direction that indicates a positive response. Green is a healing color, and visualizing this healing going from the pendulum to your friend is an important part of the process. Allow your friend to relax for a minute or two before getting up.

After the chakra balancing, your friend should feel revitalized and full of energy. After having their chakras balanced, many people say they feel better than they've felt in years. You'll also be pleasantly surprised to find that you'll also feel revitalized after performing the chakra balancing.

I find it fascinating how many people open up their hearts and minds after receiving a chakra balancing. This happens even with people who are reluctant to discuss the causes of their negative feelings while the balancing is in progress.

Obviously, it's impossible to check your own chakras in the same way. However, you can ask your pendulum questions about each chakra, and repair them in the way described above. In practice, it is much better to find someone else to do this for you. However, if that is impossible, you can do it yourself.

As you're doing the chakra balancing, it is a good idea to discuss what you're doing with the person you're balancing. If possible, ask them if they have any idea what is causing the negativity. Many people will be reluctant to discuss this with you, and you need to respect that. However, even in these cases, I still mention the most common reasons for the negativity to appear in the chakra. Sometimes the problems are so deep-seated that the person may not even be aware of them. As a result, some people find it a highly emotional experience to have their chakras balanced. You need to be kind, gentle, and understanding to perform chakra balancing on someone else.

Emotional factors are the most common reasons for blockages in the chakras:

ROOT CHAKRA: insecurity, self-doubt, inability to let go of the past

SACRAL CHAKRA: self-centeredness, selfishness, problems in communicating well with others

SOLAR PLEXUS CHAKRA: lack of self-esteem, feelings of hopelessness and powerlessness

HEART CHAKRA: difficulty in expressing emotions, lack of empathy

THROAT CHAKRA: frustration, and inability to express innermost feelings

BROW CHAKRA: living in an unrealistic fantasy world. Inability to accept the world as it is

CROWN CHAKRA: Rigidity, stubbornness, and alienation from others

HOW TO CLEAR THE CHAKRAS

This exercise is designed to keep your chakras perfectly balanced and in harmony at all times. It can be done in a matter of minutes, and is a good exercise to start the day with.

Copy the text below onto a sheet of paper, and hold your pendulum over it. Allow it to swing in a clockwise direction as you read or say the words of the script. You can modify or change these words to suit your particular needs:

> "I ask the Universal Life Source to guard and protect me all day, no matter what I do or where I go. I ask for your protection at home, at work, and while I am traveling from place to place. I ask that honesty, integrity, and harmony be part of everything I'm involved in today, and that I retain a positive outlook in every situation I find myself within.
>
> "I also ask that my chakra system remains in perfect balance and harmony throughout the day, and helps me act in every situation for the highest good of everyone involved.
>
> "I ask that my activities today benefit everyone I come into contact with, and that my aura remains bright, vibrant and full of energy throughout the day.
>
> "I allow my pendulum to continue making clockwise circles until my chakras are balanced, all negativity has been released from my body, and all fear, doubt, and worry has faded away and disappeared. Thank you for all the blessings in my life."

Once you've finished reading the script, continue suspending your pendulum until it stops, or changes direction. It is important that you do not stop as soon as you've finished saying the words, as it can take time for the ideas to be accepted. Once your pendulum stops or changes direction, thank it, and carry on with your day.

HOW TO BALANCE IDA AND PINGALA

Ida and pingala are the two nadis that run parallel to sushumna, the central nadi, and the spine. This breathing exercise, known as nadi sodhana, clears and balances ida and pingala, and also energizes the seven main chakras. Balancing ida and pingala is a six-step process.

1. Sit down comfortably in a straight-backed chair and place both feet flat on the floor. The angle at your knees should be approximately ninety degrees. Tuck your chin in slightly to ensure your whole spine is straight. Place the palms of your hands on your thighs, close your eyes, and spend about sixty seconds relaxing your body.

2. When you feel ready to start the exercise, raise your right hand to your nose, and close off your left nostril with your right ring finger. Use gentle pressure. Inhale slowly and deeply using your right nostril.

3. Close the right nostril with your thumb, and release the left nostril. Exhale slowly through your left nostril, and continue exhaling until all the air in your lungs has been released.

4. Breathe in again through the left nostril, again taking a slow and deep breath. When you have finished inhaling, close off the left nostril with your ring finger.

5. Exhale slowly and deeply through the right nostril.

6. Repeat the sequence of breathing exercises ten times.

You'll find this exercise relaxing and enjoyable. With practice, you'll find you can breathe through each nostril in turn without using your fingers to temporarily close the other nostril.

THE CHAKRAS AND CRYSTALS

For thousands of years, people all over the world have been fascinated with crystals and attributed mystical traits to them. They have been worn as amulets, and for divination, protection, and healing purposes.

The ancient Egyptians used precious stones as amulets and charms. The colors of the stones had important symbolic associations. The Egyptian *Book of the Dead* included detailed instructions on what crystals and gemstones could be used to adorn the dead. An amulet of red jasper would be placed around the dead person's neck because red symbolized blood, which related to the life force.

The ancient Greeks attributed masculine characteristics to dark colored stones, and female qualities to lighter ones. They believed amethyst would prevent drunkenness. That's why they wore amethyst amulets and drank from goblets made from amethyst.

The Romans were just as interested in crystals and gemstones as the Greeks were. The qualities and attributes of different stones recorded in Pliny the Elder's book, *Naturalis Historia*, were accepted without question until the Renaissance.

Jade was the most precious stone in China, and was considered "the essence of heaven and earth." Pieces of jade were placed in the ears and hands of dead people because they believed that this would prevent decay. Nursing mothers ate a mixture of powdered jade with honey as they thought it would improve the flow of milk.

The Chinese also used stones to indicate rank. A mandarin would wear red stones, such as ruby or pink tourmaline. His important advisers would wear coral and garnet, and officials on the third level would wear blue stones, such as aquamarine or lapis lazuli.[6]

Crystals feature in the Bible, too, and in the Book of Exodus there is a description of the jewels on the breastplate worn by the high priest:

> And thou shalt make the breastplate of judgment with cunning work; after the work of the ephod thou shalt make it;

of gold, of blue, and of purple, and of scarlet, and of fine twined linen, shalt thou make it. Foursquare it shall be being doubled; a span shall be the breadth thereof. And thou shalt set in it settings of stones, even four rows of stones: the first row shall be a sardius, a topaz, and a carbuncle: this shall be the first row. And the second row shall be an emerald, a sapphire, and a diamond. And the third row a ligure, an agate, and an amethyst. And the fourth row a beryl, and an onyx, and a jasper. (Exodus 28:15–20)

All of these stones were precious to the Jews, and were chosen because of their rarity, beauty, and value. Unfortunately, today it is impossible to tell exactly what stones were used, as in Biblical times, stones were named after their place of origin or their color.

Because gemstones come in a variety of colors, they are regularly used for chakra balancing and chakra healing. There are specific stones that are believed to be helpful and stimulating for each chakra.

ROOT CHAKRA: Red and black stones, such as fire agate, bloodstone, red calcite, carnelian, garnet, hematite, red jasper, jet, obsidian, black onyx, rose quartz, smoky quartz, rhodonite, ruby, black tourmaline, pink tourmaline

SACRAL CHAKRA: Orange stones, such as amber, red aventurine, orange calcite, carnelian, citrine, golden labradorite, opal, sunstone, thulite and orange topaz

SOLAR PLEXUS CHAKRA: Yellow stones, such as amber, ametrine, golden beryl, citrine, yellow fluorite, yellow jasper, yellow labradorite, yellow sapphire, sunstone, tiger's eye, yellow topaz, yellow tourmaline

HEART CHAKRA: Green stones, such as green aventurine, green calcite, chrysoprase, emerald, green fluorite, green jade, jasper, kunzite, malachite, olivine, peridot, green quartz, green tourmaline

THROAT CHAKRA: Light blue stones, such as blue lace agate, amazonite, aquamarine, azurite, blue calcite, blue chalcedony, chrysocolla, blue fluorite, lapis lazuli, blue sapphire, blue tourmaline, turquoise

BROW CHAKRA: Indigo or dark blue stones, such as amethyst, angelite, azurite, blue calcite, purple fluorite, iolite, indigo sapphire, sodalite, tanzanite, turquoise

CROWN CHAKRA: Clear or violet stones, such as amethyst, ametrine, angelite, charoite, diamond, mauve fluorite, lepidolite, clear quartz, selenite, sugilite, tanzanite

CHOOSING YOUR STONES

Gemstones are readily available at New Age stores, gem stores, gem and crystal shows, and over the Internet. You don't need to know anything about crystals to buy your first stones. Simply look for stones that are the right color for your purpose, and which appeal to you. Whenever I'm looking at a display of crystals or gemstones, I find myself attracted to certain stones. These are the ones I usually buy. I like to hold the stones in my hand to see what response, if any, I receive from them. Occasionally, after doing this, I might discard a stone that had appealed to me visually, but that is rare.

Once you've bought some stones, you'll need to cleanse and purify them before using them. This is because they may have been exposed to negativity before reaching you. The initial cleansing is the most important one. There are two main ways to do this.

CLEANSING YOUR STONES—METHOD ONE

Place your stones in a container of salt water for at least thirty minutes. (However, do not do this with malachite or amber, as they are damaged by salt water.) After this, rinse the stones in flowing water, and allow them to dry in sunlight. If the weather is bad, you can dry them with a soft cloth. Your stones are now ready for use.

CLEANSING YOUR STONES—METHOD TWO

This method should be used if you feel strong negative energies coming from any of the stones. Bury the stones in a bowl of salt and leave them there for three days. After this, rinse them in flowing water, and allow them to dry in sunlight.

PURIFYING YOUR STONES

The initial cleansing is the most important cleansing your stones will need. However, especially if you are using your stones to help other people, you'll need to purify them regularly.

One effective way of doing this is to lay the stones out in sunlight and leave them there for an hour or two. If possible, sit with your stones, and allow the sunlight to release any negativity you may have trapped inside your body while it also releases any negativity attached to your stones.

Another good way to purify your stones is to breathe over them. Take several deep breaths, and visualize yourself breathing in pure life-giving air. Hold the final breath for a few moments, hold the stones in the palm of your hand, and slowly exhale by breathing over them.

A third method is to hold your stones in your cupped hands. Send love and gratitude to them through your hands, your heart chakra, and the expression on your face. This method realigns the stones back to you and your energies.

If you're fortunate enough to own a crystal cluster, place your stones on this when you are not using them, and they will always be purified and ready for use.

HOW TO USE CRYSTALS
TO BALANCE YOUR CHAKRAS

You'll need eight small stones: one stone of the appropriate color to represent each chakra, and an eighth stone to act as a grounding stone. This stone can be of any color, but I usually use a green stone for this.

Wear loose-fitting clothes and make sure that you will not be disturbed for at least twenty minutes. Remove any watches, rings, or other metal objects you may be wearing. If you wish, you might play some gentle meditation music. The room should be pleasantly warm.

1. Lie down on the floor or bed and take several slow, deep breaths to help get into the right state of mind.

2. Place the grounding crystal below your feet, and then position each crystal over its respective chakra. The crystal that represents the crown chakra should be placed immediately above your head.

3. Close your eyes and take three more slow, deep breaths.

4. Relax your body as much as you can.

5. Focus on the crystal lying over your root chakra. Imagine and visualize it healing, balancing, and revitalizing your root chakra.

6. Repeat with all the other chakras, allowing as much time as necessary for each one.

7. After doing this, lie quietly for a minute or two. When you feel ready, open your eyes, and remove the stones one at a time, starting with the crown chakra and working your way down to the root chakra.

8. Lie down again, and stretch your legs to touch the grounding stone. Remain in contact with it for about sixty seconds, and then get up. (If you wish, you can hold the grounding stone for sixty seconds, instead of touching it with your feet.)

This entire exercise will take about fifteen minutes, and will balance and harmonize all the chakras. This is the way I prefer to do it. However, if you are aware that a particular chakra is out of alignment, you can lie down and place the particular stone over the chakra that you wish to energize.

HOW TO USE CRYSTALS TO BALANCE OTHER PEOPLE'S CHAKRAS

1. Ask the other person to lie down comfortably and close his or her eyes. It makes no difference if they lie down on their front or back.

2. Position yourself by the other person's feet. Ask him or her to relax by taking several slow, deep breaths. Synchronize your breathing, and take several deep breaths to center yourself and to get ready.

3. Gently place the seven stones on the chakra positions on the other person's body.

4. Sit down quietly and meditate for ten to fifteen minutes.

5. When you feel the time is right, slowly remove the stones, one at a time, starting with the crown chakra and finishing with the root chakra.

6. Give the other person the grounding stone to hold while you gently rub his or her feet and lower legs to help the grounding process.

7. Ask the person if he or she is ready to open his or her eyes.

8. Once the person's eyes are open, wait a minute or two before suggesting he or she sit up.

9. Give the person a glass of water and something to eat.

Everything you have read so far has helped you become familiar with auras, and what they do. You are now ready to start learning how to see them. That is the subject of the next chapter.

5

HOW TO SEE THE AURA

IF YOU'VE PRACTICED the exercises on feeling the aura in chapter 2, you'll already have gained a great deal of aura consciousness, and may have started seeing auras. However, it takes practice to become proficient at seeing auras, so even if you are seeing them already, you'll benefit from experimenting with the exercises in this chapter.

Interestingly, even if you haven't seen an aura yet, you actually have, although you don't realize it. Have you ever looked at someone and thought, "Why is she wearing green? That color doesn't suit her." I'm sure you've also looked at someone and thought, "She looks beautiful in that outfit. That color suits her perfectly." In both cases, you made the judgment based on the person's aura. The first person's choice of color clashed with her aura, while the second person chose a color that harmonized with her aura.

Some people start seeing auras clairvoyantly when they begin working with them. This usually occurs when they are feeling the aura. These people may well be seeing the aura through their third eye, rather than through their eyes. Sometimes it's hard to explain exactly how you are seeing the colors of the aura, as sometimes I feel I'm seeing them intuitively, while at other times I'm certain that I'm seeing them through my eyes.

This is why two people looking at the same aura can, on occasions, see different colors. Neither is wrong. This also explains why different books on aura reading sometimes contain conflicting advice. Each author is teaching the art of aura reading based on his or her experience. You are likely to come up with your own ideas and techniques as you gain expertise and experience.

Even if you have started seeing auras, go through these exercises in order, as each new exercise builds on the previous ones.

EXERCISE ONE

Sit down comfortably in a softly lit room. Ensure that any bright lights are behind you, as you do not want any light shining into your eyes. Relax your body as much as possible.

Place the tips of your forefingers together and gaze at them for about ten seconds before slowly moving them apart. You'll notice a fine, almost invisible thread of energy that stretches and remains connected to the two forefingers even though you're slowly separating them. The first time you do this, you'll probably find that the link disappears once your fingers are about half an inch apart. However, with practice, you'll find the link remains visible even when your fingertips are four or five inches apart.

If you have any difficulty in seeing the line of energy, dim the lights slightly and hold your fingers over a light-colored surface. A sheet of white paper works well for most people, but some people prefer a darker background because they see the stream of energy as being almost white in color.

Once you've succeeded once, you'll find you can repeat the exercise any time you wish, in any type of situation.

Try the experiment again, using all four fingers of each hand. You'll notice streams of energy joining all the fingers.

If you are doing this exercise with your partner, see if you can see the streams of energy connecting his or her fingertips. This means you'll be seeing someone else's aura for the first time.

You can experiment further by touching your friend's fingertips with yours, and then slowly drawing them apart. It's fascinating to see the streams of energy joining you and your friend together, even though your hands are separated. If you can, do this experiment with as many people as possible and notice the differences you'll experience when you perform this experiment with people you like and people you dislike. You'll find that the streams of energy stretch much farther with people you like. This is because your aura reaches out to encompass people you like, but does the opposite with people you do not enjoy spending time with.

Once you're able to perform this experiment successfully whenever you wish, you may like to experiment with a larger group. Seat everyone around a circular table that has a dark surface or dark tablecloth. Ask everyone to place both their hands on the tabletop with their fingers pointing toward the center. Dim the lights, and ask everyone to relax and see if they can see a fine network of lines crossing the table and connecting their fingertips with the fingertips of the person opposite them.

Be patient. It might take five minutes before anyone sees anything, but once one person sees it, everyone will. The pattern produced by everyone's fingertips creates a cat's cradle of interweaving strands of energy that crisscrosses the table. I've found this a good way to interest people in auras, as most people will not have experienced this phenomenon before.

EXERCISE TWO

The second experiment involves seeing part of your own aura. You need to do this exercise in a room with a plain-colored wall, ideally white or cream. Make sure that no lights are pointing in your direction. Dim the lights and stand several feet away from the wall, facing it.

Extend your right arm, and raise your hand so your fingers are pointing toward the ceiling. Spread your fingers slightly, and look at the wall through them. Focus on the wall rather than your hand. After a few moments, you'll notice that your fingers and hand have a distinct gray, almost colorless, haze around them.

Once you see the haze, focus on it, rather than the wall. The haze is likely to disappear when you do this. If this happens, focus on the wall again until it reappears, and try again. When you become used to seeing the haze, and can gaze at it without it disappearing, look at your fingertips. You may see fine streams of energy radiating away from them. Look at the haze surrounding your hand and notice how it is constantly moving.

This haze is your aura. Some people feel disappointed when they first see their aura, as it seems virtually colorless. There is no need to be concerned if this happens to you. It takes time to gain color awareness, and most people see auras as virtually colorless at first.

If you normally wear glasses, you should experiment with them both on and off. Many people who wear glasses find it easier to see auras when they're not wearing them.

Experiment with your other hand, and then repeat the exercise under different lighting conditions, and with different backgrounds. Dim lighting is best when you first start experimenting, but in time you'll be able to see auras under any type of lighting condition.

You should also experiment with other parts of your body. Because clothing restricts the aura, you'll find this easier to do naked or semi-clothed.

EXERCISE THREE

This exercise involves your partner. Ask him or her to sit two or three feet away from a plain-colored wall. Ask your friend to meditate, pray, or do anything else that helps to achieve a quiet, relaxed state of mind. This causes the aura to expand and become brighter, making it easier to see.

Stand back several feet, and look in the direction of your friend while focusing on the wall behind him or her. Remember a time when your eyes felt incredibly tired and heavy, and try to recapture that feeling while continuing to gaze at the wall behind your friend. Breathe slowly and deeply.

Initially, it might take a minute or two to suddenly become aware of a hazy aura surrounding your friend. It is likely to disappear as soon as you focus on it, but will return once you start looking at the wall again. You may find it helpful to close your eyes for a few seconds, and then half open them, as if you're waking up from a deep sleep. This helps you achieve the almost unfocused gaze that enables you to see the aura. Continue doing this until you're able to see the aura clearly. Notice how it seems to be in constant motion. You'll also notice that it will disappear momentarily every time you blink.

Once you've become aware of the aura around your friend's head, scan the rest of the body to see if you can see the aura everywhere else. You may find it easier to move your head, rather than your eyes, while doing this. If you move your eyes, you're likely to refocus them. This causes the aura to disappear until you reach the almost unfocused state again.

You will probably see your friend's aura around his or her neck and head, but be unable to see it anywhere else. There are two reasons for this. Clothing will constrict the aura, making it more difficult to see. Also, the mental energy emanating from the head makes this part of the aura easier to see.

Once you have become familiar with your friend's aura, move forward slowly until you can touch it. It will likely take several attempts before you can do this, as the aura is likely to disappear every time you move forward. This is caused by the changing focus of your eyes. Each time the aura disappears, return to your starting point, wait a few seconds until the aura reappears, and then try again.

Naturally, the sensations you experienced when you learned how to feel the aura will be the same, but now you'll be able to both see and feel it at the same time. This enables you to notice how your friend's aura will initially move away from the pressure of your fingers, but will then allow your fingers to enter it. The sensation is similar to pressing the surface of a balloon, but unlike a balloon, you can see your hand moving through the surface and into the aura.

Ask your friend to remove as much clothing as he or she is comfortable with. Examine the aura in different parts of your friend's body. Notice how the aura moves in a variety of ways at different parts of the body. Pay special attention to the areas close to the chakras, and see if you can detect the increased energy they produce.

Repeat this exercise at different times of the day, under different lighting conditions. Experiment outdoors as well, especially in the early morning or late afternoon. Make sure the sun is behind you. You will notice that your friend's aura will expand outdoors in the fresh air.

This exercise works best when both people are relaxed and approach the experiment with a sense of fun. Grim determination makes it impossible to see the aura. It is also best to spend maybe fifteen minutes at a time on this experiment. Several short sessions always produce better results than two or three lengthy ones.

The colors may seem disappointing when you first start seeing auras. Usually, the aura will seem gray, bluish, or almost colorless. However, with practice, the colors will become more and more visible.

EXERCISE FOUR

Many methods have been developed to help people see auras. This method involves expanding your peripheral vision. Stand two or three feet away from your partner and gaze at his or her forehead. Gradually expand your peripheral vision, starting with left and right, and following this with up and down. You'll notice that once your peripheral vision is extended as far as possible in every direction, your gaze will become slightly unfocused and you'll notice a faint haze around your friend's head. Continue focusing on your peripheral vision until the haze transforms itself into a distinct aura. Wait about thirty seconds, and then focus on the aura. As with the other experiments, the aura is likely to disappear when you first try this. Repeat the exercise as many times as necessary, until you are able to clearly focus on the aura.

EXERCISE FIVE

This is a more elaborate version that combines experiments three and four. Start with your friend standing two or three feet away from a plain-colored wall. Stand several feet away from him or her and gaze at your friend's nose. Expand your peripheral vision as far as you can above and to the left of your friend. Make a mark on the wall at that position. Return to your starting position and repeat the exercise, this time marking the spot as far above and to the right that you can see with your peripheral vision. Repeat twice more, marking the positions that are below and to the left and right of your friend.

Return to your starting position and stare at the mark you made above and to the left of your friend. Gaze at it for several seconds, and then focus on the mark that is below and to the left of your friend. Stare at this for several seconds and then look at the mark that is to the right and below. Stare at this for several seconds, and then gaze at the mark above and to the right for several seconds. While still gazing at this mark, allow your peripheral vision to expand until it includes the three other positions you had been focusing on. As you do this, your friend's aura will become visible. As with the other experiments, you might need to do this several times before you can focus on your friend's aura.

EXERCISE SIX

It's now time to see if you can see auras around strangers. Visit a shopping mall, or any other place that is likely to be busy, with your friend. Walk several paces behind your friend and see if you can see his or her aura under these conditions. Do not be disappointed if you can't. A busy environment, full of distractions, is quite different from a quiet room in your own home. Swap places and see if your friend can see your aura.

While you are there, see if you can see auras around other people in the mall. This is easier if the main source of light is behind you, and the person is framed by a clear background. Obviously, this is not always possible. You do not need to stare. Focus several feet beyond the shopper and see if you can spot the aura with your peripheral vision. Once you can do this, examine the auras of people in different situations. You'll be able to tell someone's mood. Shopping malls are wonderful places to see the auras of people who are excited, happy, sad, angry, tired, bored, in love, or stressed out.

You may feel slightly disappointed when you first start seeing auras, as they'll probably appear as a faint, colorless mist that surrounds the body. However, as you continue to practice, the colors will gradually appear and you'll be amazed that you weren't able to see them before. Be patient. Some people start seeing colors almost as soon as they see their first aura. For other people, it can take days or weeks. You'll probably see the color gray first, followed by a pale blue. Once you start seeing these, the other colors will gradually appear. They may seem washed out or dull to begin with, but gradually the colors will become more vibrant.

THE GROUND COLOR

Once you start seeing colors, you'll notice that one color tends to dominate the aura, both in size and intensity. This is known as the ground color, and is arguably the most important color in the aura because it shows what the person should be doing with their life. Naturally, if someone is doing what he or she is supposed to be doing in this incarnation, this person will have a large, glorious, and vibrant aura. For those who have not figured out what they should be doing in this lifetime, the ground color will appear dull and have less intensity. If the person knows what life path to take, but for some reason, chooses not to do it, his or her ground color will be pale and not extend far from the body.

With practice, you'll be able to tell a great deal about the quality of the person whose aura you are looking at. Ideally, the ground color should be large in size, appear rich and vibrant, and seem almost luminous in appearance. This denotes an honest person who knows what he or she should be doing in this lifetime, and is working toward achieving that goal. On the other hand, someone who is dishonest will have a small aura with colors that appear murky.

Most people have average auras that are neither rich nor murky. These people get through life as best they can, without great ambitions or goals. One of the sad things you'll notice when looking at auras is the huge amount of potential that everyone wastes. None of us achieve more than a minute amount of our potential. Fortunately, some people realize at some point in their lives that they are capable of achieving much more than they are currently doing, and take steps to improve themselves. This increased drive and motivation will be clearly reflected in their auras.

MEANINGS OF THE GROUND COLORS

Every aura is different, and you'll find it a fascinating and enlightening experience to examine and interpret them. Here are the main colors you're likely to find inside an aura:

Dark Red

People with a dark red ground color in their aura are down-to-earth, practical, hard-working people. They enjoy hands-on occupations and are usually manually dexterous. They enjoy physical work, and need to be active to feel happy. They also usually like sports, and enjoy participating in games that are physically demanding, such as weightlifting, boxing, football, or hockey.

They enjoy life and love challenges, especially ones that use their heads and hands. They are conservative, cautious, family-minded, and have a strong need for security, especially financial security.

They have strong emotions that can cause sudden outbursts of temper. These can be violent, but fortunately never last for long. They are usually mystified that other people remember these outbursts and sometimes find it hard to forgive them for what they said and did in the heat of the moment. The main lesson these people have to learn is to express their emotions in positive ways.

Red

Red is a physical color that symbolizes passion, enthusiasm, excitement, and energy. People with red as their ground color are motivated, outgoing, ambitious, and unbelievably persistent. They are also likely to be self-centered, materialistic, and impatient of anything that stands in the way of their goals. They possess a strong desire for success and will do almost anything to achieve it. Because they are single-minded, assertive, and passionate about everything they do, they usually achieve their goals.

These people need exciting, varied, and interesting work to be happy. They are curious, and want to know everything about any subject that interests them. However, they get bored and frustrated easily if their work is not stimulating and engrossing.

People with a red ground color possess huge reserves of stamina and energy, which helps them achieve their goals. However, the need to be constantly on the go makes it hard for them to slow down and relax. They enjoy physical exercise, and this is one of the main ways they use to get rid of some of their energy.

When these people use their ground color positively, their auras are a beautiful, clear red. This means they're warm, strong, kind, stable, and motivated. However, if the red is murky and unattractive, these people are impatient, irritable, and hard to please.

Orange

People with an orange ground color are positive, optimistic, sociable, considerate, and thoughtful. They are prepared to work hard and long to achieve their goals, and enjoy sharing their successes with family and friends. Although they get along well with others, they have a strong independent side and frequently end up in leadership roles. However, they have a creative side, too. This may appear as some form of expressive endeavor, such as art, music, or writing, but may well appear as a creative approach to problem solving, or the ability to come up with new, and different, ideas. They enjoy thinking, planning, and then acting. They are also good at finishing what they start. They enjoy using both their intellect and physical dexterity.

People with an orange ground color enjoy social activities, especially in the company of good friends. They are generous, open, and caring with their friends, but sometimes find it hard to understand the needs and feelings of others. This becomes easier for them once they become attuned to their own, often suppressed, feelings and gain understanding of their emotional natures.

When they're using their ground color positively, their auras are strikingly beautiful. These people are creative, practical, and enjoy making the most of every opportunity that presents itself. It is rare to find a negative aura with an orange ground color. People who reveal a dull, almost brown, ground color overindulge their base passions, and are likely to be stressed and suffering from exhaustion.

Dark Yellow

A dark yellow aura is sometimes hard to discern, and can initially appear to be almost orange or brown. People with a dark yellow aura are confident, well adjusted, and analytical. Because of this, they make their way through life one step at a time, ensuring everything has been accomplished at each stage, to avoid problems later. They're extremely patient and avoid risk as much as possible. They set worthwhile goals, but are in no hurry to reach them, as they know that "slow and steady wins the race." Adhering to this credo can sometimes frustrate others, as each minute detail has to be analyzed and discussed, usually at great length.

Although they have deep feelings, these are only ever revealed to people who are close to them. They enjoy detailed, technical, and logical conversations, and find it hard to talk about their emotions. Often their emotions are deeply repressed, so they don't have to deal with them. They also find it difficult when other people become emotional, as they prefer to deal with everything in a clear and rational manner.

They usually have good brains, and enjoy work that makes use of their good memory and love of detail. Because they're also ambitious and persistent, they almost always end up in a position of responsibility and importance.

They enjoy system and order, and always have set routines, at home, as well as at work. They need to consider new ideas for a long time before grudgingly accepting them.

The major lesson people with dark yellow auras have to learn is to become emotionally open. When they do, usually late in life, they continue to make good use of their logical brains, but also allow their intuition to finally reveal itself.

Yellow

Yellow is an enthusiastic, friendly, sunny, outgoing color. People with a yellow ground color possess good minds and enjoy coming up with new and fresh ideas. These ideas may not last long, but are important at the time. They are good conversationalists who are able to discuss almost any subject at a superficial, light level. They find it hard to be serious for long. They are sociable, easy to get along with, and generally worry-free, unless the concern is major. They have a wonderful sense of humor, and an almost childlike sense of the ridiculous. They are spontaneous, generous, and loving. They are always popular because they laugh frequently and are always fun to be around. They love entertaining and being entertained.

They are creative, but often dabble in a variety of fields, instead of focusing on one. They are versatile, and often find it hard to select one out of the many opportunities they find everywhere they go.

People with a yellow ground color find it hard to sit down and do nothing. They love being active and on the go and tend to fidget and become uncomfortable when forced to sit quietly for any length of time. Their body language is always expressive, and it is easy to tell when they are bored or unhappy.

When they use their ground color positively, the aura is radiant and beautiful. These people are happy, well adjusted, and enjoy communicating with others. However, people who have a yellow ground color that is unpleasant to look at are critical, timid, and egocentric.

Green

Green is a healing color, and people with green as their ground color are caring people who are concerned about the health and well-being of others. Consequently, they often gravitate toward a humanitarian type of career, such as teaching, medicine, or social work. They are open, friendly people who are easy to get along with and enjoy the company of others. Although they appear placid and calm, they are stubborn when they feel it's necessary—once their minds are made up, it can be very hard to change them. They are hard-working and prepared to work hard and long to achieve their goals. However, they are not obsessive workaholics—they also enjoy spending time with friends and family, and find ways to do so. They are responsible, loyal, and honest. Although they are sociable, they need plenty of time on their own to recoup their energies.

People with a green ground color find it easy to express their emotions, and make no effort to repress or hide them. This openness helps them achieve the harmony and balance they require to feel totally happy.

When people use their green ground color positively, their auras appear bright and expansive. These people are harmonious, well balanced, ambitious, and easy to get along with. However, people with a green ground color that appears dull and murky are indecisive, unhappy and find it hard to achieve their goals.

Blue

Blue is the color of freedom and variety. People who have blue as their ground color enjoy travel, excitement, and new opportunities. They have a fear of being hemmed in or restricted. Blue also indicates honesty, sincerity, confidence, and the potential to grow spiritually and intuitively.

People with a blue ground color are loving, supportive, and always ready to help and support others. Because of this, other people can easily take advantage of their good nature. They express their emotions freely, and may avoid sad movies as they cry easily. They are naturally intuitive and work best when they act on their hunches.

When people use their blue ground color positively, their auras are stunningly beautiful. These people are loyal, adaptable, honest, and approachable. However, people with a blue ground color that is small and dull are introverted and find it hard to trust others. No matter how difficult a situation may be, they find it impossible to ask for help.

Indigo

People with an indigo ground color in their auras are peaceful, calm, and accepting. They have a desire to help and nurture others, especially people close to them. They are natural humanitarians and often choose caring careers to help satisfy this need to help and assist others. They work best in harmonious environments with a small group of like-minded people with whom they can freely discuss spiritual and philosophical matters.

They are highly sensitive and possess significant spiritual and psychic potential. They seek hidden truths and enjoy learning and discovering the mysteries of life. This gives them a unique slant on life, which is often expressed through some form of creativity or unusual, even eccentric, interests.

When people with an indigo ground color use it positively, their auras appear unruffled and serene. They are tolerant, understanding, and free of stress. However, people with an indigo ground color that appears dull and shrunken, have a negative outlook on life, and tend to withdraw from others.

Violet

Violet is a spiritual color and people with a violet ground color are highly evolved spiritually. They have access to unique solutions and insights. They are sensitive, creative, and charismatic. They have the ability to subtly and gently motivate and inspire others. They have visions of a perfect world, and are frequently disappointed that other people often cannot see their view of how life should be. Education is a lifelong interest for these people, and they are always interested in new ideas and concepts. They are seldom happy with anything they achieve, as they seek perfection in all things.

Although they sometimes appear distant and aloof, deep down they are passionate, sensitive, and loving. They need plenty of time on their own to think, meditate, and make plans. They also need time to study and to develop spiritually.

If they are using their ground color positively, the aura appears almost like pure velvet. These people have considerable charisma and are seekers after truth. However, people with a violet ground color that appears dull and unappealing find it hard to accept their spiritual natures, and fight against it. These people are obsessive and are likely to have an addictive personality.

RADIATING COLORS

As your aura vision develops, you'll become aware of different colors radiating outward through the aura from the person's body. At one time, I thought the radiating colors came from the person's chakras, but they radiate outward from all over the physical body. The radiating colors reveal the person's interests and motivations (in addition to the core personality traits the ground color indicates).

The radiating color always adds strength to the ground color. For instance, a green radiating color (hard work) enhances a red ground color (attainment). Sometimes the colors appear to conflict. Someone with a yellow ground color (sociability and logic) might find it difficult early on in life to handle a violet radiating color (introspection and intuition). However, this person's natural ability to communicate will enable clear explanations of what he or she learned while developing inwardly. If the radiating color is the same as the ground color, it may be hard to detect until you examine the movements inside the aura. A few people have two or more radiating colors, and the strength of these need to analyzed before interpreting them.

Red

People with red as a radiating color are ambitious, goal-oriented, and persistent. They have an original approach that makes them good at coming up with ideas. Although they enjoy starting new projects, they often find it hard to see them through to completion. They possess leadership qualities, and are confident, capable, and enthusiastic.

If the red is murky, it is a sign of egotism, self-centeredness, and laziness.

Orange

People with orange as a radiating color are sensitive, intuitive, friendly, diplomatic, and tactful. They like people and are adaptable and easy to get along with. They are modest about their own achievements, and enthusiastic about the successes of others. They are good with details, and enjoy work that cannot be mastered easily.

If the orange is murky, it is a sign of apathy, timidity, and insecurity.

Yellow

People with yellow as a radiating color are open, friendly, loving, and enthusiastic. They are generous, creative, and enjoy all forms of entertainment. They have a natural gift at communicating with others, and often work in a field that involves their skills in this area. They are full of ideas, but don't feel impelled to act on them, although they are capable at motivating and inspiring others.

If the yellow is murky, which is rare, it is a sign of superficiality, moodiness, and gossip.

Green

People with green as a radiating color are practical, capable, responsible people with a down-to-earth approach to life. They are well organized, patient, and determined. They are conscientious, reliable, and willing to work hard to achieve worthwhile goals. They are good with details and take pride in their work.

If the green is murky, it is a sign of frustration, stubbornness, and an inability to see the forest for the trees.

Blue

People with blue as a radiating color are talented, versatile, adaptable, and forward-looking. They are enthusiastic and make the most of every opportunity. They are capable and work well with others. They enjoy challenges, and work best in fields that contain plenty of variety and change.

If the blue radiating color is murky, it is a sign of impatience, restlessness, and overindulgence.

Indigo

People with indigo as a radiating color are responsible, caring, and conscientious. They are natural humanitarians who derive great pleasure and satisfaction from helping others. They are loyal, friendly, loving, generous, and appreciative. Their greatest joy and satisfaction comes from their home and family lives.

If the indigo radiating color is murky, which is rare, it is a sign of stress, worry, anxiety, and overwork.

Violet

People with violet as a radiating color are highly spiritual. They are also deep thinkers who like to analyze and think matters through logically. However, they are also naturally intuitive. They have the ability to come up with unique, and frequently unusual, solutions to problems. They enjoy learning, and have the potential to become experts in their fields of endeavor. They feel things deeply, but try to operate on a logical, emotion-free level.

If the violet radiating color is murky, it is a sign of an overly critical and self-centered approach to life.

You might want to read this chapter again before starting on the next chapter. Make sure to experiment with all of the exercises, and decide which ones work best for you. The ability to see auras is important, for you are bound to experience stress, negativity, and antagonism at times. In the next chapter, you'll learn how to protect yourself from any sort of negativity by expanding and strengthening your aura.

6

HOW TO STRENGTHEN
YOUR AURA

YOUR AURA IS affected by everything that has happened to you since the day you were born. If you suffered from a major injury or sickness many years ago, the chances are that the trauma is still reflected in your aura today. You may be living in an environment with a great deal of electromagnetic radiation that you may not know about. You may work long hours and spend little time outdoors enjoying the sunlight and fresh air. You may hate your job. You may be unwell. You may live in a dysfunctional family and be constantly surrounded by stress.

All of these things, and many more, affect your aura. Over a period of time, problems of all kinds have the potential to wear you down and can ultimately deprive you of energy and zest for life. Consequently, everyone should strengthen his or her aura on a regular basis.

When your aura is strong, it automatically protects you from stress and negativity. In fact, in many ways it actually repels negative energies while attracting positive energies that can enhance your life.

YOUR PHYSICAL BODY

Oddly enough, you can start strengthening your aura by looking after your physical body. When you are in good shape physically, you have more energy and stamina. You have more zest for life and feel positive about yourself and the life you are living. All of this has a beneficial effect on your aura, which will expand and glow as a result.

Make sure you get some exercise every day. A brisk walk in a park or by a large body of water is especially beneficial because the air in these places is full of oxygen that will cleanse your aura while you enjoy your walk. Walking also gives you time to think about your life and what you want to achieve in the future. It's a good time to make plans and to think matters through. Make sure you think positive thoughts while you're walking. Leave any problems at home. If you find yourself thinking about your concerns while out walking, tell yourself you'll worry about them later and deliberately switch your thoughts and think about something positive.

It doesn't matter what sort of exercise you do. It all nurtures your physical body, and this overflows into your aura.

Exercise is just one part of nurturing your physical body. You also need to fuel it with good quality food. Eat plenty of fresh fruit and vegetables, and as much as possible, eliminate sugar and highly processed foods. I recently started growing my own vegetables, and was pleasantly surprised at the many benefits this provides. It gets me outdoors in the fresh air, provides me with moderate exercise, and enables us to eat fresh vegetables. I also receive enormous pleasure watching my garden flourish.

Exercise and good food are essential. You also need to ensure that you receive enough sleep, and allow sufficient time for relaxation. I've been told that people, on average, sleep for one hour less a night now than people did at the start of the twentieth century.

Spend time with people you like. Have you ever noticed how your spirits rise when you're in the company of good friends? Your aura will also react in the same way, by growing and expanding to encompass the special people in your life.

Be careful with alcohol and, if possible, avoid recreational drugs. A drink or two can help you relax, but overconsumption of alcohol will deplete your energy in both your body and aura.

YOUR EMOTIONAL BODY

Your emotional state is clearly indicated in your aura. If you are stressed, depressed, or hanging on to emotional pain from the past you will not be happy, and your aura will be weak.

It's impossible to be truly happy in the here and now when you're carrying around baggage from the past. Stresses and pressures in the present also affect your happiness and have an immediate effect on your aura.

Fortunately, there are ways to eliminate the hurt, pain, and resentments from the past and present. If the concerns are serious, you should seek help from a professional psychotherapist or psychologist. For less serious concerns, you can release the baggage yourself. Here are two methods that I've found helpful.

Baggage Release Exercise

Sit down comfortably. Start by closing your eyes and taking several slow deep breaths. Relax your body as much as possible. Once you feel totally relaxed, visualize yourself sitting comfortably wherever you happen to be. Imagine the scene if you find it hard to see it in your mind's eye. Take a slow deep breath and, as you exhale, imagine your physical body morphing into a huge ball of wool or twine. However, the ball is not perfectly round, as strands of wool are going off in all directions. All of these strands lead to emotional baggage that you are carrying around. You'll know what baggage some of the strands lead to but may not be aware of the others. Fortunately, you don't need to examine them to eliminate them from your life. Imagine you're holding a huge pair of scissors, and cut off all the loose strands until, finally, the ball of wool is perfectly round. Admire the perfectly round ball for a few moments, and then take another deep breath. As you exhale, allow the ball of wool to morph back into your normal shape and size. Spend a few moments relaxing and enjoying the knowledge that you've released all the unnecessary baggage that you no longer need. When you feel ready, take a few slow, deep breaths and open your eyes.

Although you can release most forms of baggage with this exercise, you can't remove your family. This is because family ties are strong and the connections run deep. The various members of your family are with you in this incarnation so you can all learn valuable karmic lessons. Karma relates to all of your actions, both positive and negative, in this, as well as previous, lifetimes. The important lessons you are meant to learn from your family will not be learned in this lifetime if you exclude them from your life.

Black and White TV Exercise

This is an interesting way to change the way you look at events from the past. Before starting the exercise, think about a specific event in which you felt hurt, embarrassed, ashamed, or felt you hadn't handled the situation as well as you would have liked to.

Sit down in a comfortable chair, close your eyes, take a few deep breaths, and relax all the muscles in your body. Once you feel fully relaxed, visualize an old-fashioned black and white television set in your mind. Whatever you visualize will be perfect for you. People visualize in different ways. Some people clearly see whatever they are visualizing in their minds. Others receive a faint picture. Others sense what it is, rather than seeing it.

Once the old television set is in your mind, turn it on and watch the event from your past. Watch it in a detached, unemotional manner, almost as if the experience was happening to someone else.

When the scene is over, mentally move the television set to one side and replace it with a huge cinema screen. Watch the scene again in glorious color on the large screen. The only difference is that, this time, the scene is played out in exactly the way you would have liked it to have happened in real life.

After watching the event on the cinema screen, turn to the black and white television and watch the original scene again. Notice that the picture has become fainter than it was before, and the television set appears to have shrunk in size.

Watch the scene on the cinema screen again. Afterward, watch the original event on the television set yet again, and notice that the scene is becoming hard to see as the image has become even fainter and the television has shrunk to a miniature size. Watch the scene on the cinema screen as many times as you wish. Between each run-through, switch to the television set until it has become so small and the image so faint that you can hardly see it. Say goodbye to it, and allow it to disappear from your mind. Watch the revised version again on the cinema screen. This version is your new reality, and you need never again be bothered by memories of the old version.

When you feel ready, take three slow, deep breaths, become aware of the room you are in, and open your eyes. Lie peacefully for a minute or two before getting up and continuing with your day.

AURA STRENGTHENING

You can, and should, strengthen your aura any time you feel the need. It is, for instance, a good idea to strengthen your aura before undertaking any arduous, physical task, when you feel lacking in confidence, or when you know you will shortly be in a difficult or uncomfortable situation. It's also useful to strengthen your aura before sitting for an exam, or at any other time you want your mental faculties to be at their peak. Once the reason for strengthening your aura has passed, you should strengthen, or recharge, your aura again.

There are many ways to strengthen your aura. Probably the simplest is to spend time outdoors in pleasant surroundings. You might sit beside a river or go for a walk in a park. You might spend time gardening or admiring some beautiful flowers. You might go for a swim or a bike ride. Spending time in pleasant surroundings cleanses and strengthens your aura.

Another method is to spend time with a loved pet. Stroking a cat or playing with a dog are both excellent ways to strengthen your aura. There have been numerous studies attesting to the health benefits of owning a pet. As far as I know, none of them have commented on the beneficial effects it has on the auras of both the pet and the owner.

Laughing out loud is another highly effective way to strength your aura. Watching comedies or standup comedians on TV is a good way to release tension while simultaneously cleansing and strengthening your aura.

Spending fun times with family and friends also strengthens and expands the aura. Your aura is strengthened any time you feel happy and positive about life.

Pursuing a hobby or sport also strengthens your aura. Singing and dancing are also highly beneficial. Any form of movement is helpful.

Helping others is one of the best ways to strengthen your aura, and it also strengthens the aura of the person you are helping. Any act of generosity, compassion, or love enhances your aura. It is impossible to give of yourself without receiving rich rewards, such as satisfaction, in return.

Taking time out to relax or meditate also strengthens the aura. Most people are so busy that they neglect to take time out for themselves.

As well as these everyday activities, there are practical techniques that have been devised specifically to strengthen the aura.

Physical Aura Strengthening Exercise

This enjoyable way to strengthen your aura is especially useful if you are about to perform something strenuous or athletic. I especially enjoy the sensation of feeling my aura as I do this. You can do this exercise at any time, but it is best to do it while wearing loose-fitting clothes.

Stand with your feet slightly apart and your arms loosely by your sides. Gently shake one leg, while standing on the other. If you can't balance on one leg, you can hold on to a support while doing this. Repeat with the other leg.

Move your hips in a circular motion or from side to side. Follow this by lifting your shoulders up and down. Shake your arms and hands, and gently move your neck in a slow circular motion.

Close your eyes and take three slow, deep breaths before raising your arms as high as you can. Your palms should be open and face ahead of you, and the fingers in each hand should be touching each other.

Slowly bring your arms and hands down until they are parallel to your thighs and the palms are facing backward. As you bring your hands downward, you'll probably feel your aura in your palms.

Slowly bring your arms and hands up again until you are reaching as high as you can. Pause, take a few breaths, and slowly bring your arms and hands down again. Repeat several times.

The key to success is to lower and raise your arms and hands as slowly as possible.

Visualization Aura Strengthening Exercise

This exercise is a guided visualization that uses your thoughts to strengthen your aura. As you know, positive thoughts strengthen your aura and negative thoughts weaken it. Most people have no idea how many positive thoughts they think every day, compared to the number of negative thoughts they have. Consequently, it is important to deliberately think as many positive thoughts as possible. This bolsters your confidence and self-esteem while also strengthening your aura.

You should allow about thirty minutes the first time you experiment with this exercise. With practice, you'll be able to do it in a matter of minutes, if necessary. Perform this exercise in a warm room. Wear loose-fitting clothes, and make sure you'll not be disturbed.

Sit or lie down comfortably. Take several slow, deep breaths. Focus on your breathing, and silently say, "relax" each time you exhale. Allow your body to relax completely. I usually do this by focusing on my feet and toes, allowing them to relax. Then I gradually shift my attention upward, relaxing every part of my body until finally I am completely relaxed from the top of my head to the tips of my toes.

Once you reach this peaceful, relaxed state, imagine a beam of pure white light descending and entering your body through your crown chakra at the top of your head. Each time you inhale, you breathe in more of this pure, healing energy. Each time you exhale, this wonderful white light spreads to every part of your body. Continue breathing slowly and steadily while you visualize this pure white light filling your body until you can consume no more.

Continue bringing in more white light, but now imagine the overflow leaving your body through your solar plexus chakra until you are completely surrounded by this pure, white light. Imagine the white light spreading farther and farther around you until the room you are in is completely full of white light.

Once you reach this stage, forget about the white light, and simply enjoy the pleasant feelings of total relaxation in your body, mind, and spirit. You are totally protected by this invisible light, and have all the strength necessary to handle anything that may occur in your everyday life. Your aura is now strong, energized, glowing, and large.

When you feel ready to return to your everyday life, take three slow, deep breaths, become aware of your surroundings, and open your eyes. Lie quietly for a minute or two before getting up and continuing with your day.

EMOTIONAL PROTECTION

Our emotions can be a mixed blessing. They can provide us with unbelievable happiness and joy, but also take us to the depths of despair. This exercise is designed to protect you when you are experiencing emotional difficulties with someone close to you. This person may live a long way from you physically. In fact, he or she may even be dead.

Sit down quietly and relax. When you feel totally relaxed, visualize a pure white light descending from spirit and totally filling your physical body with divine love and protection. Imagine this white light surrounding you as well, so that you and your aura are totally within the light. Spend as much time as necessary to imagine or visualize this scene.

Once it is clear in your mind, visualize a gleaming, stainless steel tube that entirely surrounds you and your aura. The only opening is at the top, and this is to allow immediate access to more white light and spiritual protection, if necessary.

Picture yourself safe, and totally protected from any form of attack, be it psychic, verbal, or physical. Hold this image for as long as possible, and silently say thanks for the divine protection, as you let the image go.

Take three slow, deep breaths, open your eyes, and think about the visualization for a minute or two before getting up. Repeat this visualization every day until you feel strong, grounded, and full of energy again.

How To Protect Your Aura

Negativity is a fact of life, and there is no way to avoid it entirely. Fortunately, you can make yourself immune to all negativity, as soon as you become aware of it, by protecting your aura. This process is also called "sealing the aura," and involves surrounding yourself with an impenetrable shield that repels all negativity, no matter where it comes from.

This protection is created consciously, and it will become more effective each time you practice it. There are a number of ways to seal your aura.

The first method is for occasions when you need to protect yourself instantly. All you need do is visualize a protective shield that completely surrounds you. Some people like to imagine that they're drawing the shield over themselves, starting from the ground, as if covering themselves with a huge invisible blanket. Once this protective shield has been drawn, it will provide protection for up to thirty minutes. It is a good idea to visualize this protective shield every day for at least a week. This practice will enable you to create a shield in a matter of seconds if you ever have to. Each time you visualize this shield, it will become stronger than before, making it more effective.

Another method is to imagine you're surrounded by pure white light. Mentally tell the white light to protect you at all times. Once you have created this imaginary protective aura, it will protect you as long as you send out thoughts of positivity, cooperation, and love. It will disappear as soon as you send out any negative thoughts. Once you become aware of this, you can draw the white light protective aura again.

Yet another method is to imagine you're holding a powerful magic wand that projects a pure white flame. Visualize yourself holding the wand out in front of you and turning in a complete circle to surround yourself with this flame. Visualize the flames flaring up and protecting you in all directions.

The final method is to visualize each exhalation of your breath strengthening and expanding your aura to create an impermeable shield of protection. Any time you feel the need for additional protection, all you need do is breathe more air into your aura.

Like anything else, the more you practice these forms of protection, the more effective they'll become. In time, you'll be able to create a wall of protection around you whenever you feel the need for it.

CLEANSING YOUR AURA

You will have more energy and zest for life if you keep your aura cleansed. There are many ways to do this. Probably the easiest method is to imagine that your aura is cleansed and glowing with vibrant health. You can do this any time you are doing a meditation or visualization exercise.

The more usual way to cleanse the aura is with your hands. Start by silently saying to yourself that you are about to cleanse your aura, and give your reasons for doing so. You might want more energy, for instance. You may feel nervous, unwell, agitated, stressed, or unhappy. It makes no difference what your reason is, but it is helpful to put a name to it before you start cleansing your aura.

If possible, perform this exercise outdoors, in sunlight. Obviously, that is not always possible, and you can perform it anywhere. Make sure the room is pleasantly warm, and there are no distractions.

Cup your hands, and stroke or brush your aura, starting at the top of your head. With a flicking motion, sweep the energy away from your body. Imagine that you're eliminating tired, old energy, and making room for new, healthy and energizing energy.

Once you have swept your head and shoulders, move down the front of your body, all the way to your feet. Repeat on each side of your body, and finally sweep both arms. Flick both hands vigorously several times to eliminate any negativity, and wash your hands thoroughly with soap and warm water.

How To Cleanse Your Aura with Incense

Incense and smudge sticks are readily obtainable from New Age stores. When lit, they produce an abundance of smoke that can be used to cleanse the aura. Make sure you buy good, quality incense. Since it doesn't matter which one you choose, make sure to select one you like. Sage is especially good for purification purposes, and is what I usually use.

Start by lighting the incense or smudge stick, and allow it to give off some smoke before starting. Most people enjoy the smell of incense, but because some people find it acrid and unpleasant, you may want to do this exercise outdoors. Make sure you have a supply of water handy, in case of accidents. I've never had a problem, but always make sure to have a supply of water, as well as solid dishes and containers to hold and contain anything that involves fire before starting.

It's easier to do an incense cleansing with a partner, but you can do it on your own if necessary.

Stand with your legs slightly apart and your hands by your sides. Close your eyes, and take slow, deep breaths while your partner cleanses your aura.

After you have taken a few deep breaths, your partner will start moving the smoking incense around your body, holding the stick approximately twelve to eighteen inches away from your body. There is no set way of doing this, but it is usual to start with the head and gradually work downward. The first time I received an incense cleansing, my friend started at the top of my head and slowly spiraled the incense down my body in a clockwise direction until she reached my feet. After a brief pause, she spiraled her way up to the top of my head again. In my innocence, I thought this was the only way in which it could be done, but this is definitely not the case.

Your partner should use his or her intuition, and perform the cleansing in the manner that feels right at the time. Consequently, he or she may cleanse one side of the body and then the other. Or your partner might opt to thoroughly cleanse the area around the head, followed by the arms and trunk, and finally the legs.

You'll feel purified and full of energy after having your aura cleansed in this way. You will also gain peace of mind and a sense of tranquility, calmness, and contentment.

If you're using this method to cleanse your aura on your own, you need to keep your eyes open, as it is potentially dangerous to perform this cleansing with your eyes closed.

AURA STRENGTHENING CRYSTALS

Ideally, your aura should be strong at all times, providing you with feelings of strength and confidence. Unfortunately, though, there are many reasons why your aura could be weakened. These include illness, geopathic stress, electromagnetic pollution, prolonged stress, psychic attack, overwork, and mental or emotional difficulties.

Fortunately, there are remedies for all of these. Quartz is found all around the world and is extremely useful for cleansing and healing the aura. Holding a quartz crystal in front of your solar plexus chakra will immediately strengthen your aura. Quartz can also be used to enhance psychic ability, stimulate the immune system, dissolve fear, and detect and repair any breaks in your aura.

How To Repair Breaks in the Aura

Sit down in a straight-backed chair with an amethyst, carnelian, citrine, quartz, or green tourmaline crystal in your hand, with the point protruding between your thumb and index finger. Close your eyes, take a few slow, deep breaths, and then slowly run the crystal over your body, starting with the area around your head. Any breaks in your aura will feel cold and lacking in life and energy. Hold the crystal over the break until it feels warm and reenergized. Continue scanning your body until you have completed your arms, legs, front, and sides. You will need to stand up, with your eyes closed, to scan your back, buttocks, and thighs.

It is easier to do this exercise with a partner, but you can also do it on your own.

CRYSTALS TO PROTECT YOUR AURA

There are several crystals that are useful in protecting the aura. They can be worn as jewelry or carried in a purse or pocket.

AMBER: Amber cleans and revitalizes the aura. It also balances the physical, mental, emotional, and spiritual bodies, and wards off negativity.

AMETHYST: Amethyst cleanses and purifies the aura, and attracts divine energy. It can also be used for repairing breaks in the aura.

APACHE TEAR: Apache tear absorbs negative energies of all sorts.

BLACK JADE: Black jade wards off negativity.

BLOODSTONE: Bloodstone cleanses the entire aura, but is particularly beneficial for the etheric body.

CITRINE: Citrine cleanses and harmonizes the aura.

GREEN TOURMALINE: Green tourmaline wards off negativity, repairs breaks in the aura, and provides protection.

JET: Jet wards off negativity coming from other people.

LABRADORITE: Labradorite helps keep the aura large and strong by preventing any leakage of energy.

MAGNETITE: Magnetite is used to strengthen the aura, and is particularly beneficial for people recovering from illness.

QUARTZ: Quartz is an excellent crystal for all forms of aura protection. It cleanses, strengthens, and protects the aura. It also repairs any breaks in the aura.

SELENITE: Selenite releases any negativity that might be held inside the aura.

CRYSTALS AND PSYCHIC ATTACK

A psychic attack occurs when someone wishes you harm. Most psychic attacks are not intentional, but they can be done deliberately if someone wants to hurt you. A psychic vampire is someone who gains energy by draining energy from other people. Again, this is not normally done deliberately. However, it can be extremely debilitating for the person who has been attacked.

Most nondeliberate psychic attacks are created by other people's envy, jealousy, or hate. Occasionally, someone may wish you harm and deliberately attack you psychically. If you're healthy and your aura is strong, your aura will be able to withstand all but the most prolonged and determined attacks.

Fortunately, a number of crystals can help you protect your aura from all forms of psychic attack. The most powerful crystal for this is black tourmaline. Amber, ametrine, carnelian, fire agate, and fluorite are also useful sources of protection. Selenite provides protection from psychic vampires.

When your aura is strong you'll feel energetic, confident, and in control. Consequently, it's important to pay attention to the well-being of your aura. A strong aura can help ward off illness and disease. Your aura also plays an important role in healing whenever you are unwell. That is the subject of the next chapter.

7

THE AURA IN
HEALTH AND HEALING

COLOR HAS ALWAYS been used in healing. The ancient Chinese used color when diagnosing different health conditions. The Egyptian Papyrus Ebers, dating from c.1550 BCE, listed many colorful cures, such as white oil, red lead, wool dyed indigo, and verdigris, a green copper salt that was used to cure cataracts. The ancient Greeks used Tyrian purple, obtained from shellfish, to cure boils and ulcers.

The ancient Greek Doctrine of Humors was a complete medical system based on the four elements of fire, earth, air, and water. The four elements, or humors, were associated with different colors, qualities, and body fluid:

AIR: Sanguine Hot and moist red blood

FIRE: Choleric Hot and dry yellow spleen

WATER: Phlegmatic Cold and moist white water

EARTH: Melancholic Cold and dry black bile

Any imbalances in the humors, which were revealed by color variations in the person's complexion, urine, or excrement, were a sign of health problems. The Chinese, Indians, Greeks, and Romans all used versions of the Doctrine of Humours.[1] This doctrine remained the foundation of Western medicine until the eighteenth century.

Avicenna (980–c.1037) was a renowned physician and author of many books, including *The Canon*, which described his research of color healing. He claimed that yellow reduced inflammation and pain, and that blood pressure could be raised with red and lowered with blue.

During the Renaissance, Paracelsus (1493–1541) used color as a major part of his work as a physician.

By the nineteenth century, there was very little interest in color healing, as knowledge of anatomy and the increased use of drugs meant doctors placed emphasis on diseases of the physical body over holistic healing.

Fortunately, the pioneering work of two American physicians, Dr. Seth Pancoast and Dr. Edwin Babbitt, created a new interest in color healing. Dr. Pancoast had studied the wisdom of the great philosophers, and based much of his work on their researches. His book, *Blue and Red Lights*, published in 1877, described how he used red and blue filters in his work. His technique was deceptively simple. He passed sunlight through panes of red or blue glass. He wrote: "To *accelerate* the Nervous System, in all cases of relaxation, the *red* ray must be used, and to *relax* the Nervous System, in all cases of excessively accelerated tension, the *blue* ray must be used."[2] Dr. Pancoast also filtered water through colored glass to create a healing drink.

Just one year later, in 1878, Dr. Babbitt published *The Principles of Light and Color*,[3] which sold well all around the world, and is still in print. Dr. Babbitt invented the Thermolume, a special cabinet that used natural sunlight. He found this too limiting, however, and built another cabinet that used an electric arc.

In the early twentieth century, Dr. Rudolf Steiner (1861–1925), the celebrated occultist, philosopher, and teacher, took an interest in color. He believed every color had spiritual significance and felt they would play a major role in medicine in the twenty-first century. Dr. Steiner worked mainly with what he called "active colors" (red, blue, and yellow), and "image colors" (green, white, black, and peach blossom).

Interest in color healing continued to grow throughout the twentieth century. In 1934, American physicist Dinshah P. Ghadiali published his three-volume work, *Spectro-Chrome Metry Encyclopedia*.[4] This was a home-study, color healing course that is still available today.

Dr. Harry Spitler, a doctor and optometrist, developed a system of color therapy called syntonics, in which light is applied directly through the eyes. In 1977, Jacob Liberman, an American optometrist, heard Dr. Spitler speak, and began his own research. His system of healing is called "ocular phototherapy." Jacob Liberman's major book on the subject is called *Light: Medicine of the Future*.[5]

In 1979, Dr. Douglas Pratt of the University of Minnesota proposed a scientific basis for color healing. He had been researching the effects that colored lights had on different plants, and discovered that very deep red colors sped up the growth of plants, while very deep blue colors did the opposite. He suggested that if these colors worked this way with plants, they might also do the same for humans.[6]

There is a well-documented case of cancer being healed by the spectral colors of sunlight. In 1982, Dr. Helen Fleming, head of Radiologic Technology at Merced Community College in California, was diagnosed with an advanced case of lymphatic cancer. Her oncologist recommended chemotherapy and radiation therapy, but Dr. Fleming turned that down, as she had seen firsthand the effects caused by this treatment. Instead, she took a leave of absence from her work, and moved out to the country where she was able to take nude sunbaths outdoors in complete privacy. Dr. Fleming believed that she could cure the cancer by absorbing spectral colors. She sunbathed regularly, and the tumor disappeared.

However, the tumor returned after she returned to Merced College and resumed working under fluorescent lights. Dr. Fleming asked John Ott, a well-known color and light researcher, to install a device called the Ott-Lite, which simulates sunlight, at her home, office, and lecture room. Again, the tumor disappeared, and when she died many years later, it was from a heart attack, not the cancer.[7]

Energy healers are able to detect irregularities and changes inside the aura. This was demonstrated in an interesting experiment conducted by Dr. Susan Wright that was published in the *Western Journal of Nursing Research*. She asked a number of Therapeutic Touch practitioners to examine fifty-two patients who were suffering from chronic pain to see if they could locate areas of energy field disturbances. The practitioners assessed the energy fields of each patient with their hands and reached a significant level of agreement about where the pain came from.[8]

Most health problems appear inside the etheric body. Healers are able to sense health problems from the past, as well as current sickness, and even future sickness, by examining the quality of the etheric double.

Energy healers believe they can pick up problems well before the patient is aware that anything is wrong. This means that they can rebalance the person's energy fields and restore him or her to perfect health before any sign of the illness has manifested. Caroline Myss is one of many medical intuitives who are able to diagnose health problems without the need for possibly dangerous or invasive medical procedures.

There are many varieties of energy healing available today. These include: Pranic Healing, Psychic Healing, Reiki, Spiritual Healing, Subtle Energy Healing, and Therapeutic Touch.

Mental health problems, such as schizophrenia, are also indicated in the aura. They are revealed by an unusual shape and lack of symmetry in the aura as a whole.

HEALING WITH THE CHAKRAS

As each chakra relates to a specific part of the body, any imbalances in the chakras can indicate potential illnesses and other health problems. Being aware of this can prevent illnesses from occurring, as remedial action can be taken well before the illness manifests itself.

Here are the parts of the body that relate to each chakra:

ROOT CHAKRA: (Red) The skeletal system, muscles, and the immune system. The adrenal glands.

SACRAL CHAKRA: (Orange) Bladder, kidneys, uterus, ovaries, testicles, and prostate.

SOLAR PLEXUS CHAKRA: (Yellow) Lower back, digestive system, and the pancreas.

HEART CHAKRA: (Green) Heart, lungs, thymus gland, and immune system.

THROAT CHAKRA: (Blue) Shoulders, arms, and neck. Thyroid gland.

BROW CHAKRA: (Indigo) Eyes and pituitary gland.

CROWN CHAKRA: (Violet) Central nervous system. Pineal gland.

EXERCISES FOR THE CHAKRAS

These exercises are intended to open the chakras, and fill them with vital energy. They also stimulate and energize all of the organs associated with each chakra. The exercises should be performed in sequence, starting with the root chakra and finishing with the crown chakra.

Root Chakra

Visualize the color red while performing this exercise. Stand with your feet wide apart and knees slightly bent. Move upward and downward a few times. Finish by rocking backward and forward with your knees bent.

Sacral Chakra

Visualize the color orange as you perform this exercise. Stand with your feet apart and your knees slightly bent. Place your hands on your hips. Slowly move your body in a circular motion. Do ten clockwise circles, and follow it with another ten performed counterclockwise.

Solar Plexus Chakra

Visualize the color yellow as you perform this exercise. Stand with your feet slightly apart and jump up and down several times. If necessary, ask someone to hold your hands while doing this.

Heart Chakra

Visualize the color green while performing this exercise. Stand with your feet slightly apart, and stretch your arms above your head. Hold this position and take in a slow, deep breath. Exhale slowly, and stretch your arms out to the sides. Hold this position for several seconds. Repeat three times.

Throat Chakra

Visualize the color blue while performing this exercise. Start by moving your head slowly from side to side several times. Once you have done this, slowly rotate your head in a clockwise direction several times. Repeat in a counterclockwise direction. Finish by rolling your shoulders while quietly humming a song you enjoy.

Brow Chakra

Visualize the color indigo while performing this exercise. While facing straight ahead, move your eyes up and down, and to the left and right. Follow this by looking upward to the left, downward to the right, upward to the right, and downward to the left. Repeat with your eyes closed. Finish by gently rubbing the area between your eyebrows with the first and second fingers of your dominant hand.

Crown Chakra

Visualize the color violet while performing this exercise. Place your right hand on the top of your head, and rub your scalp several times in small clockwise circles. Follow this by using both hands to give yourself a scalp massage. Finish by rubbing your scalp in clockwise circles with your right hand.

COLOR BREATHING

Color breathing is an excellent way to revitalize and balance the chakras by inhaling all the colors of the rainbow. Alternatively, you can use the same breathing technique to inhale the color you need, and then visualize it going to the affected part of your body. If, for instance, you were suffering from headaches, you could sit down quietly and visualize indigo energy entering your body each time you inhale, and then spreading throughout your head to cure your headache.

The technique is simple to learn and can be performed anywhere, at any time. Start by focusing on your breathing, taking slow, deep breaths, holding it for a moment or two, and then exhaling. After taking several deep breaths, imagine a pure white light descending from above and filling your entire body with its healing energy. Visualize this for as long as you can. Once the image starts to fade, focus on your breathing again, and imagine you're absorbing the specific color you need for healing each time you inhale.

There are different ways to visualize the colors entering your body. Some people visualize the color or colors entering through the nose as they inhale. Others imagine the color entering the body through the chakra that relates to the particular color. Some people visualize red, orange, and yellow energy entering the body through the feet. They picture green and blue entering the body through the heart chakra, and indigo and violet entering through the top of the head. It makes no difference which method you prefer.

You do not need to hold your breath for lengthy periods when doing color breathing. Visualize the color coming in when you inhale, hold the breath for a second or two, and then exhale.

STRENGTHENING THE CHAKRAS

The following exercises are useful ways to stimulate and strengthen the various chakras. However, you should not do any of these exercises without medical supervision if you are suffering from any problems with your heart, eyes, or blood pressure.

Root Chakra

Walking is an excellent exercise for the root chakra, as each step you take strengthens your connection to the ground. If you are not used to walking, start with short walks, and gradually increase the duration. If possible, go for walks in beautiful surroundings, such as in a park or along the seashore.

Another method to strengthen the root chakra is to sit on a straight-backed chair with both feet flat on the ground. Push downward with your thighs. You'll notice a slight sensation in the perineum, between the anus and genitals.

Sacral Chakra

Dancing is the perfect exercise for the sacral chakra, especially if it is done to strong, repetitive, and rhythmic music. Belly dancing is ideal, but it makes no difference what movements you make. You may prefer to practice this on your own. Many people feel self-conscious when they first start moving their hips and pelvis in time to music.

Solar Plexus Chakra

Slow stretches are an excellent way to strengthen your solar plexus chakra. Grab the thumb of one hand with the fingers of your other hand, and stretch your arms above your head, trying to get the biggest stretch you can.

You can also go down onto your hands and knees and rock backward and forward.

Heart Chakra

Any exercise that increases your heart rate will strengthen the heart chakra. Another exercise is to take several deep breaths into your diaphragm, between your lungs and stomach, and then sing out loud. It makes no difference if you can sing in tune, or not. If you can't sing in tune, find a place where you can sing to your heart's content without anyone else hearing you. If you can't find anywhere else, do your singing in the shower.

Throat Chakra

A useful exercise to strengthen the throat chakra is to sit in a straight-backed chair and slowly lower your head onto, or close to, your right shoulder. This stretches the left side of your neck. Follow this by lowering your head to the left shoulder to stretch the right side of your neck. Repeat several times.

It can also be helpful to gently massage each side of the neck from just below the ear to the shoulder.

Brow Chakra

Any physical activity that also requires thought is good for strengthening the brow chakra. A sport, such as tennis, is a good example, as you need to remain focused on the game. Yoga and tai chi are also good ways to stimulate the brow chakra.

Crown Chakra

Lying on a tilt board or some other surface that has your feet higher than your head is an effective way to strengthen the crown chakra. Start by lying in this position for about two minutes. Over time you may choose to lie in this position for up to five minutes.

CRYSTAL HEALING

Crystals have a beneficial effect on the mind, body, and spirit. Because they help people relax, they are particularly useful for stress-related problems, such as headaches.

Pink and green stones are helpful for encouraging physical relaxation, while yellow stones relax the mind, and purple stones raise your consciousness and enhance spirituality. Useful stones to help you relax are: amethyst, chrysoprase, citrine, blue jade, onyx, quartz (especially rose and smoky quartz), selenite, and watermelon tourmaline.

Violet stones, such as amethyst, are useful for curing headaches. Lie down on your back, and place one amethyst immediately above your head, in the area of your crown chakra. Place a second amethyst on the area of the brow chakra, immediately above the eyebrows. Close your eyes, and visualize the violet energy removing all traces of your headache. Lapis lazuli is extremely effective for migraines and cluster headaches.

Stress can be reduced with tiger's eye, rose quartz, and two pieces of clear quartz. Lie down on your back, and place the rose quartz over your heart chakra and the tiger's eye over your sacral chakra. Hold the two pieces of clear quartz loosely in your hands. Relax all the muscles of your body, and then breathe in all the colors of the rainbow, starting with red. Allow each color to travel throughout the body before gathering in the area that relates to its color.

If you are suffering from a lack of energy, lie on your back for ten minutes. Place a yellow citrine on your solar plexus chakra, and carry it with you throughout the day. Do this twice a day until your energy is restored. Other stones that can also be used to raise your energy include: aventurine, bloodstone, orange calcite, chalcedony, garnet, red jasper, rutilated quartz, ruby, and topaz.

Millions of people around the world suffer from the debilitating effects of depression. Fortunately, a number of crystals can be used to help sufferers regain their emotional balance. These include: amber, chrysolite, citrine, jet, and smoky or rose quartz.

Healing Emotional Hurts

It would be hard to find someone who has never suffered an emotional hurt. Fortunately, most people can release them and let them go within a reasonable period of time. Unfortunately, some people unconsciously hold on to past hurts, making it impossible for them to forgive, let go, and start again. This makes it extremely hard for them to give and receive love.

You can release any past emotional hurts by lying on your back and placing a piece of rose quartz or purple tourmaline over your heart chakra. Close your eyes, and quietly meditate for about ten minutes. This simple exercise will remove emotional hurts, while at the same time balance and energize your heart chakra.

A number of crystals can be worn or carried to facilitate emotional healing. Any green stone, such as green aventurine or green tourmaline, works well to harmonize and balance the heart chakra, which relates to green.

Agate is a useful stone for eliminating anger, bitterness, and resentment created by past relationships.

Chrysocolla heals past relationship problems and opens up the heart again.

Blue quartz helps people forgive anything that occurred in the past and encourages them to start looking forward to a new relationship in the future.

Rose quartz helps resolve problems caused by a broken heart by bringing peace and calm to the sufferer. It also opens the person up to experience universal love.

Purple tourmaline aligns the root and heart chakras, helping the person experience a full, loving relationship again. Purple tourmaline increases sexual energy as a useful byproduct.

Watermelon tourmaline combines the two colors associated with the heart chakra (green and pink) and enables the person to love again.

INDICATIONS OF ILLNESS IN THE AURA

Most indications of health problems show up in the etheric body close to where the physical problem is located. However, it takes time to learn if the signs you see relate to old illnesses, current problems, or problems in the near future. This is why it is extremely important that you don't diagnose health problems in other people's auras. This is irresponsible and illegal, if you don't have a medical licence. If you see a potential problem or abnormality, you should suggest the person has a medical checkup, but it is vital that you don't alarm someone with something you see in his or her aura.

Although you can't diagnose physical problems, you can help people with emotional and mental problems that are revealed in their auras.

We all have negative thoughts at times, and these briefly come and go in our auras. These thoughts sometimes contain powerful emotions as well. However, if someone constantly thinks angry or negative thoughts, this will be revealed as a murky or unpleasant area in the aura, usually around the head. The best cure for this is to help the person change his or her patterns of thinking, and become more positive. However, not everyone wants to be helped, and you must respect that.

DISTANT HEALING

You can send healing to people, no matter where in the world they happen to be. However, whenever possible, you should obtain their permission first. Even though you're doing it with good intentions, you are interfering with their free will if you send healing without permission. There are exceptions to this. If someone is in a coma, for instance, it is impossible to ask for permission. If someone is ill in a remote part of the planet, you may have no way to communicate. If you have no idea where someone is, but you know he or she is ill, you may want to send healing to help that person.

Absent, or Distant, Healing Visualization

Sit down comfortably, and spend a few minutes with your eyes closed, quieting your mind. Visualize the person you're going to send healing to, and picture him or her surrounded by an aura. Mentally ask the Universal Life Force to help you send healing to this person.

Take several slow, deep breaths, imagining that you're filling yourself up with healing energy. Send all of this energy to your heart chakra to infuse it with love. When, in your imagination, you're filled to overflowing with healing energy, direct this energy to the person you are intending to heal. Visualize a beam of green light traveling in a huge arc from your heart chakra to the heart chakra of the other person, strengthening and healing him or her.

Thank the Universal Life Force for enabling you to do this. Open your eyes, and think about what you've done for a minute or two before getting up.

If you know the color that the person needs, you can send a specific color, as well as, or instead of green. However, green and gold are both good colors to send for any type of healing.

If you are sending healing to someone you haven't met, visualize the person holding a large card that has his or her name written on it.

If you intend sending absent healing to people on a regular basis, you should prepare a special room, or space, to work in. Surround yourself with beautiful objects, such as crystals or flowers. You might choose to light candles and dedicate them to your absent healings. If possible, perform your healings at the same time each day. By doing this, you'll automatically enter the desired state of mind each time you enter this sacred space. Most people who do distant healings pray or meditate for a few minutes to prepare themselves before starting their healing work.

Regaining balance and good health is an accomplishment in and of itself. However, being healed can also be viewed as a new beginning—a point at which a person is wholly ready to take on new projects, pastimes, and employment with abandon. Most people subconsciously hold themselves back from achieving their dreams. Few people live up to their potential. Fortunately, you can use your knowledge of auras to overcome your self-imposed limitations, set powerful goals, and achieve whatever it is you desire. That is the subject of the next chapter.

8

HOW TO USE YOUR AURA TO ACHIEVE YOUR GOALS

EVERY THOUGHT YOU have, and every emotion you experience, creates vibrations that have an effect upon your physical body and your aura. You are probably more aware of the effect your emotions have on your body, but your thoughts, good or bad, also have a powerful influence upon you. In fact, much of the time, your thoughts and emotions are connected. Here's an example. If you happen to think of someone who hurt you many years ago, the actual emotions that you felt at the time will probably come flowing back, and you may feel angry or upset. Your thought created the emotion. Feelings of this sort have an immediate, measurable effect upon your body.

Because of this, you can deliberately feed your mind and body with positive thoughts that will help you to achieve your goals. Thinking positively will enhance your life in many ways, but you need to do more than simply think positive thoughts to become successful. In addition to positive thinking, you need to add emotion and visualization to feed the desire you have for the particular goal you have set for yourself.

I find it fascinating that so few people ever set goals for themselves. You have a much greater chance of becoming successful if you know where you want to go. If you have no idea what it is you want, your life will be aimless and you'll lack direction. You'll spend a great deal of time in pleasant backwaters, but will achieve nothing that propels you forward.

HOW TO SET WORTHWHILE GOALS

Most people fail to set goals, and then wonder why they don't achieve success. However, many people who do set goals for themselves also fail to achieve great success. These people achieve more than the people who fail to set goals, but sometimes it's not a great deal more. This is because average people set average goals for themselves. Average goals are good, as they're easy to achieve. You don't have to stretch yourself very much to achieve them. And it's important to set average goals for yourself as they provide pleasure and satisfaction. They can also motivate you to set further goals.

However, if you are to achieve great success, you also need to set goals that appear virtually impossible. These are the goals that make your heart race and your hands sweat when you think about them. These goals can be described as magnificent obsessions. Even if you fail to achieve these goals, you'll achieve a great deal by working steadily toward them. It's similar to the saying that says you should reach for the stars. Even if you don't get as far as the stars, you'll at least get to the moon.

When choosing worthwhile goals for yourself, strengthen your aura, and seal it from negativity. Many people think about achieving great things, but fail to do it because of inner doubts and fears. This will not occur if you strengthen and seal your aura.

HOW TO GAIN CONFIDENCE AND SELF-ESTEEM

Almost everybody feels insecure in certain aspects of their lives, and would like to have more self-confidence. Fortunately, no matter how lacking in confidence you might be at the moment, you can turn this around and gain all the confidence you need. Confidence starts with a sense of feeling worthwhile. You need to love yourself, and accept yourself as you are. You must believe in yourself. Once you believe in yourself, you'll have the confidence you need and will be able to achieve anything you set your mind on.

The chances are that you're already confident in certain parts of your life. You might, for instance, be extremely confident at work, but find social situations difficult. You might be confident in most areas of your life, but feel terrified when asked to speak in public. I know a man who makes his living as an auctioneer, and is able to entertain and sell while at work, but is unbelievably insecure and shy in his personal life. An acquaintance of mine is in his early fifties, but has never had a girlfriend because he lacks confidence when in the company of women. However, he is confident and successful in his career.

Your mind is both your best friend and your worst enemy. Your mind is constantly giving you both positive and negative messages. If you pause and evaluate them every now and again, you might be surprised to discover how many negative messages you give yourself. We are all much harder on ourselves than we are on anyone else. When you become aware of your negative thoughts, you have a choice. You can continue to think negatively, which means you'll probably have a lousy day. Or you could turn them around and deliberately start thinking positive thoughts. Another possibility is to stop believing the negative thoughts. Just because they come from your mind doesn't mean they're true.

Here's a useful exercise that will help you eliminate problems from the past that are affecting your confidence and self-esteem today.

You'll need to set aside about thirty minutes. Make sure the room you're working in is pleasantly warm, and that you will not be disturbed.

1. Lie down comfortably, take some slow, deep breaths, and relax. I usually lie down on the floor when performing exercises of this sort. This is because I fall asleep far too easily when I lie down on a bed.

2. Take as much time as necessary to relax completely. Mentally scan your body to make sure every part is completely relaxed, and focus on any areas that are still tense until they let go and fully relax.

3. Visualize a scene from the past when you felt confident and happy. It makes no difference when this scene occurred. It may have happened recently, or possibly date from your early childhood. As you relive this scene in your mind, pay attention to the feelings and sensations that appear in your body. Naturally, you'll feel confident, but other feelings should surface, too. You may sense that you are loved and cherished by others. You may feel a sense of ease and relaxation. You'll certainly feel extremely happy. Take note of everything you feel and sense as you relive the scene.

4. Visualize this scene again, but make the colors even more vibrant than they were before. Spend as long as you wish in the scene, absorbing everything you can.

5. Now visualize a scene from your past where your confidence let you down, or you felt you had not made a good impression. Watch the scene until the end. If you felt embarrassed, humiliated, or angry when the situation actually occurred, you may feel these emotions in your body again. Allow the scene to carry on until the end.

6. You now have two different experiences and two different emotional responses. Relive the first scene again, the one in

which you felt confident and able to achieve anything. Make it as vibrant and as vivid as possible.

7. Switch to the second scene, but, if you can, keep the emotional responses you received from the first scene. Continue to go through the second scene, the one in which your confidence let you down, but notice that your response is quite different, as you have retained all the energy and enthusiasm generated by the first scene.

8. Repeat steps six and seven. If you had difficulty retaining the happy, confident feelings while reliving the second scene, repeat steps six and seven until the second scene has lost all its power to affect you.

9. If you wish, you can repeat steps three to eight using another situation in which your confidence let you down. Feel proud of yourself, as from now on you're able to act confidently in any type of situation. Say to yourself: "I have all the confidence I need in every type of situation."

10. Take three slow, deep breaths. Become familiar with the room you're lying in. When you feel ready, open your eyes. Remain lying down for a minute or two, and then stretch and get up. Have something to eat or drink, and then carry on with your day.

You should repeat this exercise several times, using a different scene from your past each time. You can repeat scenes you've already looked at, if you wish. The point of using different scenes each time is to gradually change your memories of anything that might have affected your confidence in the past. Whenever you have a few spare moments during the day, picture yourself in your imagination, feeling confident and in control.

You'll find, as a result of doing this exercise that your confidence will increase. You'll feel more self-assured and in control in every aspect of your life. This will have a direct effect on your aura, which will expand and become more radiant as a result. You can enhance this even further, by adding another scene at the tenth position of the visualization exercise.

The scene, which shows you acting confidently, has just come to an end. Now imagine yourself utilizing that same sense of confidence in every area of your life from now on. As a first step, allow your aura to appear around your body, and take pride and pleasure in how large and radiant it is. Take a deep breath, and hold it while you silently say, "I am totally confident," and then exhale. As you exhale, notice how your aura expands and glows even more. You can repeat this several times, if you wish.

If you ever feel that your confidence is slipping, repeat this exercise. If you ever find yourself acting in a way that does not enhance your confidence and self-esteem, change the memory in your mind by performing this exercise. It makes no difference if the incident happened ten minutes ago or dates back to your early childhood.

HOW TO DEVELOP YOUR PERSONAL POWER

We all have our own unique personalities. When you expand your aura, you become more charismatic and powerful. Some people do this naturally, but anyone can learn how to do it.

It's a good idea to consciously expand your aura before going anyplace where it's important you make a good impression. I recently showed a young woman how to do this before going for a job interview. She got the position she was after, and I think this was partly due to her expanded aura, which gave her charisma and presence.

I have a friend who's an extremely talented stage magician. However, he has never achieved anywhere near the degree of success that his talents deserve. This is because, as soon as he gets on stage, his personality seems to disappear. This makes it impossible for him to command an audience, and people are always reluctant to come up on stage to help him. Everyone has a personality, of course, and most of the time my friend has a pleasing one. For some strange reason, his personality fades away while he's on stage. It was difficult to speak to him about this, as he was totally unaware of the problem. Fortunately, he's prepared to do anything necessary to improve his performing skills, and now he deliberately expands his aura before going on stage.

Every time you deliberately expand your aura, you enhance your personality, presence, and field of influence. You develop charisma. Have you ever watched a teenage boy speaking to a young woman he wishes to impress? Although he didn't do it consciously, he expanded his aura by putting all his focus and energies into impressing the girl.

You can do this consciously to increase your attractiveness to potential partners, and for any other purpose where you want to impress others, sell yourself and your ability, and feel confident in any type of situation. You may, for instance, want to sell yourself at a job interview. You may want to impress a potential mother-in-law. You may want to make new friends.

We covered how to expand your aura in chapter 6. However, if necessary, you can also expand your aura instantly. All you need do is take a deep breath, and visualize your aura expanding as you exhale. One exhalation might be all that is needed, but you can repeat it several times if necessary.

HOW TO CHANGE PATTERNS OF BEHAVIOR

Several years ago, I went for a long walk with a friend who was trying to lose weight. After the walk, she immediately sat down and ate a large blueberry muffin. I wasn't sure whether or not to say anything, but she must have read the expression on my face.

"I deserve it," she said. "We walked for more than an hour."

"Yes," I agreed. "The only problem is you'd probably need to walk for at least another hour to get rid of the extra calories you're getting from the muffin."

"I know," she said. "But my mind tells me I need a muffin, and I need it now. Why does my mind keep doing this to me?"

My friend is not unusual. All of us sabotage ourselves at times. My friend is trying to lose weight, but it's not going to happen if she rewards herself with large muffins every time she exercises. Consciously, she knows this, of course, but something inside her insists that she needs that muffin.

I have a neighbor who is much more disciplined. Several years ago, she gave up smoking overnight, when she started a new relationship with a nonsmoker.

"He's a very special man," she told me. "And I wanted the relationship to last. He never said anything about my smoking, but I knew he didn't like it. So I quit."

My neighbor was able to instantly give up a highly addictive habit, but my friend found it almost impossible to stop overeating. In both instances, there was a reward. My neighbor has been with her special man for several years now. That might not have been the case if she'd continued smoking. My friend felt the need for a reward after exercising, and chose blueberry muffins, even though she knew it was not a good choice. She laughed when I suggested she eat an apple instead. The blueberry muffin nurtured her in ways that an apple couldn't.

The person who gave up smoking had consciously, or unconsciously, looked at two possible scenarios. She could have continued smoking, in which case the relationship may not have lasted. The other scenario was to give up smoking and have a good chance of keeping the relationship.

My friend who was trying to lose weight had not thought about the two possible outcomes. She could continue "rewarding" herself with inappropriate foods, which meant she would never lose weight. In time, she'd probably abandon the walking, and end up heavier than before. The other possibility was to continue exercising, but to reward herself appropriately. In this case, she would probably reach her desired weight.

I'm happy to say she finally reached her goal. It wasn't easy, and she had a number of setbacks along the way. However, she reached her desired weight some years ago, and has been able to maintain it. This is the exercise she used to clarify her desired goal, and to provide the necessary motivation to continue until she achieved it.

Changing Behavior Exercise

The first part of this exercise is to identify the problem, think about why you do it, and to devise ideas and strategies about how you can change this behavior. You can do this in a number of ways. You can examine the situation while meditating or relaxing. You might discuss your problem with a trusted friend, or you could write down everything you can think of that relates to the problem. Once you've done this, and thought about it, you'll need to set aside time on a regular basis to go through a relaxation process that will help resolve the problem.

1. Lie down comfortably and relax your entire body. Once you have done this, mentally scan your body to make sure every part is totally relaxed. Focus on any areas of tension until they are relaxed, too.

2. Imagine that you are at a fork in the road and have to decide which direction to take. The road on the left is an easy road, as it means continuing your life the way it is now. The road on the right is the path you'll take if you choose to change your behavior. The path on the right can change your entire life.

3. Look at the road on the left, and visualize yourself ambling along that road several months from now. You have changed nothing. See the scene as clearly as you can in your mind's eye. Allow the feelings you have for yourself to come to the surface. If, for instance, your goal is to lose weight, see yourself even heavier than you are now.

4. Continue walking along the road on the left for about a year, and notice how this apparently easy road is becoming more

difficult and painful all the time. If, for instance, your goal is to eliminate drugs from your life, visualize what your life might be like twelve months from now. See yourself being evicted from your home and selling off your last possession to feed your drug habit. As it's important to see the negative scenario as vividly as possible, you should make it seem as unpleasant and horrible as possible.

5. Allow yourself to go back to the fork in the road, and visualize yourself as clearly as possible. Look at your small, insipid-looking aura, and realize the effects your negative behavior is having on every part of your being.

6. Take a slow, deep breath, and let that picture fade from your mind as you realize that that's not how your future is going to be.

7. Look at the road on the right, and think about your goal. Visualize yourself in a situation in the near future, once this goal has been accomplished. In your mind's eye, picture all the details, including sounds, smells, tastes, and the congratulations of others.

8. Allow your mind to place you in different situations in which you are leading a happy, successful life with your problem well in the past. Notice how happy you are. Again, use all your senses to visualize as many details as possible.

9. Visualize yourself standing at the fork in the road. Mentally see your aura, and imagine it expanding outward and glowing radiantly, as you allow your new pattern of behavior to become permanently instilled in your aura.

10. Enjoy this scene for as long as possible. Look at both the left and right roads. In your imagination, turn away from the road on the left and start walking confidently toward the road on the right.

11. Fill your mind with feelings of success. Feel proud of yourself. You're a winner. You're prepared to pay the price because you know that you are worth it, and the goal is worth it.

12. Enjoy these feelings for as long as you wish. When you feel ready to return to your everyday life, take three slow, deep breaths, familiarize yourself with your surroundings, and open your eyes.

13. Lie quietly for a minute or two, thinking about the two possible scenarios. When you get up, drink some water or eat something to ground you before continuing with your day.

You should repeat this exercise every day, if possible, until you start reaping the rewards of your success. The most important part of this exercise is to make the visualizations as vivid and emotional as possible.

Years ago, I used this exercise to help a man who had a gambling problem. When he visualized life on the road on the left, he started to cry. He remained in a relaxed, meditative state, but tears poured down his face. I knew then that his problem was virtually resolved. Afterward, he told me that he'd visualized his family losing their home and all their possessions. While he and his family were standing on the street feeling absolutely hopeless, people came and took his children away to put them in a home. He thought he'd never see them again. When he visualized the road on the right, he saw his family move into a beautiful home in a highly desirable neighborhood. They could afford the home because he no longer gambled. Again, tears ran down his face, but this time they were tears of happiness.

I believe that our emotions are much more powerful than our thoughts. Therefore, it's important to utilize both your mind and emotions in your visualizations to help you achieve your goals as quickly and as effectively as possible.

HOW TO STAND UP FOR YOURSELF

Recently, a man came to see me because he wanted to become more assertive. He had got into the habit of giving in for the sake of an easy life. Not surprisingly, he discovered people took advantage of him everywhere he went. Even at home, his partner controlled the remote to the television, and would change the program without bothering to consult him. At work he'd been overlooked for a promotion, and he put that down to the fact that he was always "too nice."

His biggest problem was the regular meetings he attended at work. Before entering the meeting room, he felt a loss of confidence and, consequently, he sat quietly and failed to put his ideas forward.

I gave him three suggestions that were intended to help him at his work meetings. As it turned out, he was able to utilize them in every area of his life.

1. The first suggestion was that he gently rub the tips of his thumb and forefinger together as he walked to the meeting room. This is a technique used by actors who suffer from stage fright. It helps them to relax and gain confidence before walking on stage. In a sense, my client was walking on stage when he entered the meeting room.

2. The second suggestion was for him to breathe in as much red energy as possible. I wanted him to breathe in so much red that it overflowed his body and surrounded him with an invisible red shield. This also gave him enough confidence to stand up for himself.

3. My final suggestion was that as he exhaled he should say to himself, "I'm assertive." I suggested that he do this at least three times before entering the room.

Any one of these suggestions would have helped, but the combination of the three made my client feel invincible. He told me a few days later that after the meeting his colleagues asked what had happened to him, as the change was so great. My client was so excited by the changes that occurred as a result of these ideas that he started using them in other areas of his life, with great success.

When I spoke to him recently, he told me, "Sometimes I feel a little bit selfish, as now I think 'what do I want to do.' In the past, I would always have gone along with whatever the other person suggested. I finally feel I'm my own person."

HOW TO BE HAPPY

Many years ago, T'ai Lau, a wise friend of mine, told me, "If you want to be happy, be happy." These simple words are amazingly profound. They show that we can be happy, no matter what is going on in our lives, if we want to be. Each of us chooses our own state of mind, moment by moment, as we go through the day.

Most of the time, people feel that happiness is out of their control. They may wake up in the morning feeling happy. However, delays on the freeway, or someone cutting them off at an intersection, can destroy that happiness in an instant, and ruin their entire day. This means that a situation that was totally out of their control dictated their level of happiness. It is much better to follow T'ai Lau's advice, and to remain unattached to occurrences that don't really matter.

Minor problems are one thing. The major problems that life brings are a different matter. How is it possible to be happy when you're faced with health problems, accidents, relationship difficulties, the sudden loss of a job, or the death of someone close to you? Obviously, when a major disaster occurs, you need to handle it as best you can. Thoughts of happiness are likely to be far from your mind. However, once the immediate situation has been dealt with, is it possible to be happy while dealing with the aftermath?

Our thoughts and emotions create vibrations that affect our auras all the time. Most of the time, these vibrations are faint ripples that appear and disappear in seconds. However, when strong emotions are attached to them, they create thought forms that remain in the aura, and affect every cell of the body. Thought forms last as long as the energy that created them remains in the person's mind. Consequently, negative thoughts and emotions that are not released can ultimately affect the health and well being of the whole body.

Here's an exercise you can do at the start of the day that will help you enjoy a happy and successful day. Write down exactly what you need to enjoy a wonderful day. You might write something like:

"With the help of Infinite Spirit, I am going to enjoy a happy day. I feel contented, relaxed, and ready to enjoy every moment of today. I am filled with positive expectations. Small things will not bother me. Large things will not bother me, either, as I anticipate happiness, and know everything will work out well for me today. My physical body feels healthy and well. It is full of life and energy. My aura is glowing with happiness and positive expectation. My aura will continue to expand and glow with every pleasant experience that occurs today. I'll greet friends and strangers alike with a friendly smile, and a positive word. Today is going to be a happy day for me, as I'm going to enrich today for everyone I come across. I'll express my thanks and appreciation for everything other people do for me. I'll take time to enjoy the beauty of my world. I'll be willing to help others in any way I can. Today is going to be a happy day. Thank you for your help."

Once you have written whatever you wish on a piece of paper, suspend a pendulum over it and allow it to swing in a clockwise direction while you read what you have written out loud. Once you have finished, the pendulum will gradually stop swinging, and this will tell you that your request for a happy day will become a reality.

HOW TO GAIN WHAT YOU DESIRE

Most people have no clear idea as to what they want to achieve in this lifetime. I read that people spend more time planning their summer vacation than they do planning the lives they'd like to lead in the future. This is a huge waste of potential, and there must be huge numbers of elderly people who are filled with regrets that they wasted their talents and lives, when they could have achieved so much more.

Self-limiting beliefs, along with fear, doubt, and worry, hold many people back. However, all of these can be overcome. It can be useful to carry pen and paper with you for a week or two. Whenever you get a spare moment, think about what you'd like to do with your life. Think about career, money, investments, love, family, travel, and spiritual goals. Each time you get an idea, no matter how far-fetched or impossible it may sound, write it down. Everyone has different goals and ambitions. My goals are likely to be quite different from yours. This is as it should be, and your goals will be right for you, and my goals will be right for me.

By the time a week has passed, you'll have a list of goals you'd like to achieve. Evaluate them all carefully, and decide if you really want to achieve them. You may, for instance, have decided to learn a foreign language. That's an extremely worthwhile goal, but you need to ask yourself if you're prepared to put the necessary time and effort into achieving it. If the answer is "no," you should remove it from your list.

You may have set goals that are not ambitious enough. If, for instance, you've decided that you want to become the foreman at your place of work, consider aiming higher. A good test is to close your eyes and think about your goal. Become aware of your body, and notice how it reacts to your goal. A worthy goal should not be too easy to achieve. You should feel a sense of nervousness or excitement in your body when you think about a goal that takes you well out of your comfort zone.

Ideally, you should end up with a list of short-term and long-term goals covering a number of different areas of your life. Some should be comparatively easy to achieve, while others will take a considerable amount of time and effort.

Once you've made a list, write them down on paper and carry it around with you. Read the list at least once a day. This is a useful thing to do whenever you are waiting in line or have a few spare moments.

You also need to imprint these desires in your aura. You know that thought forms of different sorts appear and disappear in your aura. Although this usually occurs subconsciously, you can also do it consciously. You're going to deliberately create positive thought forms inside your aura that will help you to attract and achieve your goals.

HOW TO CREATE THOUGHT FORMS

This is a ten-step process. Start by choosing one of your goals, ideally one of the more challenging ones. As you'll ultimately create thought forms for each goal you have on your list, in some ways it doesn't matter which one you start with. However, I think it's best to imprint the more important, long-term goals in your aura first.

1. Lie down comfortably and relax in the usual way.

2. When you feel totally relaxed, think about your goal. Visualize yourself, and what your life will be like, once you've achieved it. Picture yourself, happy, confident, and successful, once you've achieved it. See yourself enjoying the rewards that come your way as a result of achieving your goal. Think about how different, and better, your life will be as a result of achieving this goal. Think about these things for as long as you wish.

3. When you feel ready, bring yourself back to the present, and think about the very first step you're going to take to achieve this goal. See yourself making this first step, and allow yourself to feel proud as this is the first step toward the life you desire, and know you can achieve.

4. Once you've made the first step, think about the second step, and see yourself taking that, too. Again, feel proud and happy that you're prepared to pay the price and do whatever is necessary to achieve your goal. Continue doing this with all the additional steps that are required until you finally achieve your goal.

5. Repeat step two, and allow yourself to thoroughly enjoy the rewards that are yours as a result of achieving your goal.

6. Take a slow, deep breath, and as you exhale visualize yourself imprinting your desired goal as a thought form on your aura.

7. Picture yourself surrounded by a huge aura, in the middle of which is a beautiful shape containing all the thoughts and emotions that came to your mind as you were thinking about your goal.

8. Your goal is now imprinted inside your aura as a thought form. It will remain there, working for you, until you reach your goal.

9. Spend a minute or two quietly relaxing, content in the knowledge that your goal will become a reality, as it is permanently imprinted in your aura.

10. When you feel ready, take three slow, deep breaths, become familiar with the room you are in, open your eyes, and lie quietly for a minute or two before getting up. Have something to eat or drink before carrying on with your day.

Repeat this exercise with all your other goals. Do not try to do them all in a single day. It's better to allow a day or two to elapse before creating another thought form. Each time you add another thought form, visualize your aura in your mind, and see all the thought forms you've deliberately imprinted there.

Continue reading your list of goals every day, and picture your aura each time. When you achieve a goal, you can thank the thought form for helping you, and allow it to dissolve. You can do this by visualizing your aura, focusing on the thought form, thanking it, and allowing it to gradually fade until it disappears.

You cannot have too many deliberately imprinted thought forms, so feel free to add to your list of goals whenever you wish. However, you should always question yourself before adding a goal, as it's a waste of time and energy to create a thought form for a mere whim that you have no intention of pursuing.

HOW TO ATTRACT WHAT YOU WANT

When you create a thought form, your aura acts as a magnet that helps you attract whatever it is you desire. Of course, you'll still have to work for whatever it is, but once you've magnetized your aura, obstacles and roadblocks seem to disappear.

Part of this is because you've decided exactly what it is you want. This fact alone puts you well ahead of most people. In addition to this, while imprinting the thought form inside your aura, you went step by step through all the stages that led to your goal. Consequently, you not only decided what it is that you wanted, you also worked out a plan to achieve it. Naturally, you'll have setbacks and difficulties at times, but you'll be able to surmount them and continue onward to success.

Once the thought form has been created, you'll need to visualize it on a regular basis to keep it activated, and ensure it keeps working for you. You also need to be aware of your thoughts, as you don't want to undermine your thought forms with negative thoughts about your goal. If you find yourself thinking negative thoughts, pause, take a deep breath, and deliberately think about something happy and positive. When used properly, thought forms ensure you attract exactly what you want.

Ideally, you'll set goals in several different areas of your life. You should set financial, career, social, health, family, and spiritual goals. I know many people who have home, family, career, and health goals, but have given no thought to setting spiritual goals for themselves. Fortunately, you can use your aura to enhance your faith. You'll learn several ways of doing this in the next chapter.

9

HOW YOUR AURA CAN
ENHANCE YOUR FAITH

SPIRITUALITY HAS BECOME more and more popular in recent years. People who would never consider attending a church, synagogue, or mosque are reading books on how to live soulfully and how to lead a better life. Others are nurturing the spiritual side of their makeup in art, music, and nature. A sculptor I know says that every time he's working on a project, he is in direct contact with the Divine.

There are many different spiritual traditions, and I don't consider one to be better than another. It's helpful to learn about other traditions, as they'll bring in added elements to your own personal faith and philosophy. No matter what spiritual path you may be on, the exercises in this chapter will confirm what you already know, and may open many new areas of exploration.

MEDITATING WITH THE CHAKRAS

Meditation is a simple process that has many benefits. We all lead busy lives, and it can be helpful for body, mind, and soul to quietly sit or lie down and meditate, even for just a few minutes. Meditation reduces stress and lowers the heart rate. It helps you to focus and concentrate. It enables you to fully appreciate all the blessings in your life. Ultimately, it enables you to accept yourself and others exactly the way they are. It allows you to see life in a more open and generous manner.

In its most basic form, meditation is simply a matter of closing your eyes, focusing on your breathing, and allowing yourself to relax. Many people find it helpful to repeat a word or phrase to help them enter into, and remain in, a quiet meditative state. Any word or phrase that makes you think of peace and quiet will do. You might choose "peace," "tranquility," "stillness," "I am one with God," or "calm and relaxed." You might prefer to use a mantra, such as "Ohm" or "Rahm."

I sometimes use the phrase, "I'm peaceful and calm." I silently say this as I inhale. I hold the breath for a second or two, and then repeat the phrase as I exhale. As I do this over and over again, my entire body relaxes and I drift deeper and deeper into a meditative state.

Many people tell me they can't meditate, as they can't still the thoughts in their mind. It's natural to have thoughts in your mind, and they're going to enter your awareness every now and again, no matter how deep you are in the meditative state. The solution to this is to accept the thought, and gently let it go. Bring your attention back on to your word or phrase, and concentrate on this until another thought comes into your mind. Accept and dismiss this thought, too, and carry on with your meditation.

Like everything else, you'll become better at meditating if you practice regularly. A neighbor of mine attends a daily meditation class. She already knows how to meditate but continues going to the class because it forces her to meditate every day.

If you practice meditation for any length of time, you'll find it becoming something you look forward to. It's a special time when you can shut the world and all its concerns out of your mind, and go deeply into a meditative state.

After you've practiced meditation for a while, you'll be able to take it even further by meditating with your chakras. This is not a big step, as you may already have noticed some or all of your chakras opening when you meditate.

These meditations work with one chakra at a time. You may find meditating on a particular chakra once will provide you with all the insight and knowledge you need. You may find it necessary to meditate on the same chakra every day for a week, or even longer. You may even find a particular chakra too painful and sensitive to deal with. This will relate to a profound hurt in the past that you have not fully dealt with. If this occurs, meditate normally and ask for help in releasing it. Once you've let it go, you'll have no problems meditating with that particular chakra.

Root Chakra

Close your eyes, take several slow, deep breaths, and allow your body to relax. Once you feel totally relaxed, focus your attention on the area around the base of your spine. Allow yourself to feel the grounding energy entering your root chakra, and notice if it's powerful, slow, or lacking in energy. Take three more slow breaths, and then allow your mind to think about the qualities represented by your root chakra. How strong is your will to live? Do you enjoy physical activities? Examine the words associated with this chakra: survival, root, and power. Breathe in the color red, and allow this to gather at the base of your spine. Remain still for as long as you can and see what thoughts come into your mind.

When you feel ready to return to your everyday world, silently thank the root chakra for the insights it has given you. Take three slow, deep breaths, and become aware of the room you're in. When you feel ready, open your eyes. Remain in the position you're in for a minute or two and think about the root chakra meditation you've just concluded. When you get up, eat or drink something before carrying on with your day.

Sacral Chakra

Close your eyes, take several slow, deep breaths, and allow your body to relax. Once you feel totally relaxed, focus your attention on the area just below your navel. You'll feel a slight response when you locate your sacral chakra. Allow this chakra to open. Remember it opens in front of you, as well as behind you. Allow yourself to gently feel your sacral chakra in your mind, and see what response comes to you. Take three slow, deep breaths, and think about the functions of this chakra. How is your emotional life? Are you comfortable in your sexuality? How is your sex life? Relax quietly and see what comes into your mind. Breathe in the color orange and allow it to gather in the area of your sacral chakra. Notice what difference, if any, this makes to the chakra.

When you feel ready to return to your everyday world, close your sacral chakra slowly and gently. Send it love and silently thank it for the insights it has given you. Take three slow, deep breaths, and become aware of the room you are in. When you feel ready, open your eyes. Stay in the position you're in for a minute or two and think about the sacral chakra meditation you've just concluded. When you get up, eat or drink something before carrying on with your day.

Solar Plexus Chakra

Close your eyes, take several slow, deep breaths, and allow your body to relax. Once you feel totally relaxed, focus your attention on your stomach area. Gradually allow your mind to float over this area and hone in on your solar plexus chakra. Allow it to open, both front and back. Think about this chakra and what it does for you. When you feel ready, ask any questions you have that relate to your solar plexus chakra. You might ask: Do you feel good about yourself? How is your self-esteem? Are you happy? Do you feel positive about the future? After asking these questions, rest quietly and see what thoughts come into your mind. Breathe in the color yellow and allow it to gather in the area of your solar plexus chakra. Sense what differences, if any, the color makes to your solar plexus chakra.

When you feel ready to return to your everyday world, close your solar plexus chakra slowly and gently. Send it love and silently thank it for the insights it has given you. Take three slow, deep breaths, and become aware of the room you are in. When you feel ready, open your eyes. Stay in the position you're in for a minute or two and think about the solar plexus chakra meditation you've just concluded. When you get up, eat or drink something before carrying on with your day.

Heart Chakra

Close your eyes, take several slow, deep breaths, and allow your body to relax. When you feel totally relaxed, focus your attention on the area of your heart. This is the chakra that is most likely to be open. Gently examine your heart chakra in your mind. If it seems too open, close it slightly. If it's closed, or needs to be opened more, allow this to happen, both in front and behind you. Allow yourself to go as deeply into your heart chakra as possible, and feel safe and protected inside. Enjoy these feelings for a while, and, when you feel ready, ask yourself questions about love. Do you love yourself and others? Can you forgive easily? Do you feel you're forever giving love, but receiving little back in return? Do you respect yourself? Are you sympathetic? Do you enjoy helping others? Do you nurture yourself, and others? Listen to the answers and, when you feel ready, breathe in the color green and let it settle in the area of your heart. Notice what difference, if any, this makes to your heart chakra.

When you feel ready to return to your everyday world, close your heart chakra slowly and gently. Send it love and silently thank it for the insights it has given you. Take three slow, deep breaths, and become aware of the room you are in. When you feel ready, open your eyes. Stay in the position you're in for a minute or two and think about the heart chakra meditation you've just concluded. When you get up, eat or drink something before carrying on with your day.

Throat Chakra

Close your eyes, take several slow, deep breaths, and allow your body to relax. Once you feel totally relaxed, focus your attention on the area of your throat, and become aware of the gentle pulsing of your throat chakra. The throat chakra is the first of the Trinity, the three highest chakras. As their vibrations are finer than the lower four chakras, it may take longer to sense your throat chakra. Take whatever time is necessary to locate and sense it. Once you've found it, allow this chakra to gently open, both front and back. Gently explore your throat chakra with your mind, and, when you feel ready, ask any questions you have about this chakra and its functions. You might ask: Do I speak up when I should? Do I express myself honestly? Am I kind and understanding? Do I always work with integrity? Pause, and see what responses come into your mind. Once you've received all the information you need, breathe in blue energy and allow it to collect in your throat. Notice any changes this color makes to your throat chakra.

When you feel ready to return to your everyday world, close your throat chakra slowly and gently. Send it love and silently thank it for the insights it has given you. Take three slow, deep breaths, and become aware of the room you are in. When you feel ready, open your eyes. Remain in the position you're in for a minute or two and think about the throat chakra meditation you've just concluded. When you get up, eat or drink something before carrying on with your day.

Brow Chakra

Close your eyes, take several slow, deep breaths, and allow your body to relax. When you feel totally relaxed, focus your attention on the area between your eyebrows. Allow your attention to gently explore your forehead until you sense your brow chakra. As it's one of the three highest chakras, it might take time before you become aware of its gentle movement. Once you've found it, allow it to open, both front and back. Do this slowly and gently. Some people feel as if they're losing control of themselves when they do this. If you open them slowly, this will not occur. Enjoy the sensation of being inside your brow chakra. Take your time and explore it gently. Think about all the work your brow chakra does for you. Silently say the word, "intuition," and see what thoughts come into your mind. Think of as many other words as you can that also relate to this chakra. "Consciousness," "insight," and "truth" are good examples. Allow as much time as necessary to receive all the thoughts and insights you can. Once you've done this, breathe in indigo and allow it to collect in your forehead. Pay attention to any changes this color makes to your brow chakra.

When you feel ready to return to your everyday world, close your brow chakra slowly and gently, both front and back. Send it love and silently thank it for the insights it has given you. Take three slow, deep breaths, and become aware of the room you are in. When you feel ready, open your eyes. Stay in the position you're in for a minute or two and think about the brow chakra meditation you've just concluded. When you get up, eat or drink something before carrying on with your day.

Crown Chakra

Close your eyes, take several slow, deep breaths, and allow your body to relax. As this is the highest chakra, allow more time than usual to ensure that you're totally relaxed. Once you feel certain that you are completely relaxed, focus your attention on the top of your head. Let your mind gently move around the middle of your head until it senses the almost imperceptible energy of your crown chakra. Your crown chakra is always open, but if you feel it necessary, you can gently open it up more. Take note of anything you feel or sense as you gently examine your crown chakra. Become aware that all living things are interconnected at a deep, hidden level. Notice any spiritual or mystical insights that come to you as you sink deeper and deeper into your crown chakra. You may feel a strong connection to the Divine. All of this can be highly emotional. If it becomes too intense, mentally step back for a few moments, and then decide if you want to continue, or finish the meditation for that day. There is nothing wrong with finishing the meditation early. You can repeat it as many times as you wish, and each time you'll sink deeper into your crown chakra and gain further insights.

Complete the meditation by breathing in violet energy. Imagine it gathering at the top of your head, and notice what effect it has on your crown chakra. Take several slow, deep breaths, and visualize white energy descending on you, entering your body through your crown chakra and gradually filling your chakras, your aura and body with divine healing energy. Enjoy the sensation of this for as long as you can.

When you feel ready to return to your everyday world, send your crown chakra love and silently thank it for the insights it has given you. If you opened up your crown chakra at the start of this meditation, gently return it to the degree of openness it was at the start. Take three slow, deep breaths, and become aware of the room you are in. When you feel ready, open your eyes. Remain in the position you're in for a minute or two and think about the crown chakra meditation you've just concluded. When you get up, eat or drink something before carrying on with your day.

Do not rush through these seven meditations. It's much better to spend time meditating deeply with one chakra than it is to skim lightly over all of them. Take as much time as necessary with each chakra, and notice the profound changes that will gradually occur in your life.

PRAYING WITH THE CHAKRAS

The chakras are also useful whenever you wish to communicate with the Divine. You can do this in two ways. You can place your dominant hand over the particular chakra you wish to involve in your prayer, and then pray in your normal manner. Alternatively, you can pray while doing one of the chakra meditations.

If you wish, you can work your way through all the chakras in your prayer. Here are some suggested prayers for each chakra. You don't need to use the same words I do. You should modify and adapt them to suit your particular needs.

In particular, you should use your own name for the Universal Life Force. There are many different names for God, and rather than try to include as many as possible, I have used the words, "Divine Spirit."

Root Chakra

Divine Spirit, thank you for keeping me grounded. I'm grateful for your love and support, and for giving me courage, persistence, and life itself. Please help me release any doubts, fears, shame, and guilt I might be holding. I no longer need them, and am happy to set them free. Please help me accept all that is good, and to reject anything that takes me away from my true path. Thank you, Divine Spirit, for all the blessings in my life.

Sacral Chakra

Divine Spirit, thank you for the gifts of optimism, hope, and creativity. Help me to love and respect others, as well as myself. Thank you for the gift of sexuality. Please help me to use it in healthy and appropriate ways that enhance and enrich the lives of both my partners and myself. Thank you, Divine Spirit, for all the blessings in my life.

Solar Plexus Chakra

Divine Spirit, thank you for enabling me to feel good about myself, and to be happy about the life I am living. Help me to be contented and at ease in every type of situation. Please help me release any anger, stress, frustration, or resentment I may be carrying. I am happy to let them go. Thank you, Divine Spirit, for all the blessings in my life.

Heart Chakra

Divine Spirit, thank you for all the love I have in my life. I am grateful for all the love I receive, and am thankful that I can also express my compassion and love to others. Surrounded by love, I feel at peace, no matter what is going on in my life. Please help me recognize and appreciate the divine spark in everyone I encounter in my daily life. Thank you, Divine Spirit, for all the blessings in my life.

Throat Chakra

Divine Spirit, thank you for the gift of self-expression. Let my voice be an instrument of praise and worship. Please help me express myself openly, honestly, and tactfully at all times. Please help me see the best in others. Help me use words to express my love and understanding for all of Your creation. Thank you, Divine Spirit, for all the blessings in my life.

Brow Chakra

Divine Spirit, thank you for making me aware of my spiritual nature. Please fill me with wisdom and knowledge. Let me feel Your presence everywhere I go, both at work and at play. Let me come closer to your divine light. Thank you, Divine Spirit, for all the blessings in my life.

Crown Chakra

Divine Spirit, fill me with your divine light, and let it flow into every cell of my body. Fill me with radiance and love, and help me become the person I desire to be. Thank you, Divine Spirit, for all the blessings in my life.

HOW TO DEVELOP YOUR SPIRITUAL AURA

With practice, many spiritually evolved people have been able to discern several layers in the aura:

1. The Etheric body

2. The Astral body

3. The Mental body

4. The Higher Mental body

5. The Spiritual body

6. The Solar body

7. The Cosmic body

The sixth and seventh layers are usually detectable only on people who are highly evolved spiritually. They are seen as bands of brilliant, white light.

As music speaks directly to your soul, all of the different layers are affected by music. The spiritual layer is particularly affected by wind chimes, high notes played by string instruments, and harp and organ music.[1]

Your spiritual devotions will be enhanced by playing music involving these instruments before, or during, your meditations and prayers. There will be times when you wish to pray in silence, and you should avoid music on those occasions. However, most of the time, you'll find that playing a peaceful piece of music that you enjoy before your devotions will quiet your body, mind, and emotions, allowing the Divine to communicate directly with your soul.

Playing music before your prayers should be regarded as part of your spiritual time. Make yourself comfortable, and listen to the music quietly and reverently. You may find that different pieces of music affect different chakras. This is a sign that a particular chakra is craving more energy. You can do this by closing your eyes, taking several deep breaths of the color relating to the particular chakra, and sending it to the chakra.

The music you choose to play is entirely up to you. You might play, *Stars and Stripes Forever* by John Philip Sousa, if you wanted to enhance your physical aura. Here are some possibilities you can use to enhance your spiritual aura:

Florida Suite by Delius

Nimrod (from the *Enigma Variations*) by Elgar

St. Cecilia Mass by Gounod

Vespers of the Blessed Virgin by Monteverdi

Ave Verum Corpus by Mozart

Requiem Mass by Mozart

Pope Marcellus Mass by Palestrina

Prelude to Act 1 (from *Lohengrin*) by Wagner

I prefer listening to classical music, especially chamber music, before praying. I also prefer music that I won't find myself singing along to, as I find that far too distracting. Consequently, I wouldn't play *Memory* (from *Cats*) by Andrew Lloyd Webber, even though a close friend plays it almost every time she prays. Experiment with different pieces of music until you find the right pieces for you.

Once you've completed your prayers or spiritual meditation, you should remain seated quietly for a minute or two before carrying on with your day.

With a strong spiritual side to your being, you'll realize you have the potential to achieve anything. In the next chapter, you'll learn how to use your aura to achieve great success.

10

WHY BE AVERAGE?

Every person on this planet is special. In fact, everyone is much more than that. Everyone is a miracle. Life itself is a miracle, and we should all be making the most of this incredible gift we've been given by leading lives full of wonder and fulfillment. Sadly, this is the exception, rather than the rule.

By most standards, my dentist was a success. He made a great deal of money, and invested it wisely. His wife and children adored him. Yet he was never totally happy, as he hated being a dentist. In his office he displayed magnificent photographs he'd taken, and he dreamed of giving up dentistry and becoming a professional photographer. Sadly, he died without achieving this goal. Although he achieved worldly success, he never did what he really wanted to do. He was an average dentist, but he had the potential to be a great photographer.

I know many people who are coasting through life. They do enough to get by, but seldom plan ahead or look for opportunities to progress. They might sometimes dream of having plenty of money, wonderful relationships, fulfilling and satisfying work, exotic vacations and vibrant health, but are not prepared to do anything to make these goals a reality.

There are many reasons why people fail to use their innate talents and skills. Lack of motivation is a common reason. Fear is another. However, the most important reason why people fail to be anything other than average is a lack of self-belief.

Most of what happens to us in life is the direct result of what our minds believe. People who believe in themselves know they can achieve their goals and become successful. People who lack self-belief know that even if they take the first step toward a goal, they'll ultimately fail. Of course, as they believe they'll fail, that is exactly what happens. People who believe in themselves frequently experience numerous failures before achieving success. Nevertheless, because they believe they can become successful, they pick themselves up and try again and again until they reach their goals. People who lack self-belief fail to do this, and feel life is somehow fighting against them. They're the people who constantly say self-defeating messages, such as: "I never get a break," "I'm too old to get a promotion," and "I can never make ends meet." Because they believe these statements are true, they become their reality.

Fortunately, even if you've got into the habit of filling your mind with negative thoughts, you can turn your life around by changing your belief system, and start filling your mind with positive thoughts. Once you start doing that, you'll change your life.

SELF-BELIEF EXERCISE

This is a pleasant meditation that you can do any time you wish. Before doing it, you need to make a list of the attributes you want to gain. You might, for instance, want to think more positively. You might want more confidence, and the ability to stand up for yourself. Write down everything you can think of, no matter how insignificant or ludicrous they may seem.

Once you've done that, think about the traits you'd like to eliminate. Think about the qualities you'd like to replace them with, and add them to your list. If you're timid now, for instance, you might write down that you want to be brave.

It makes no difference how long or short your list is. Once you've completed it, number the items in order of importance. Associate a color with each trait you want to develop. Here are some suggestions:

RED: Energy, enthusiasm, confidence, assertion, self-esteem, strength

ORANGE: Physicality, comfort, security, persistence, determination

YELLOW: Emotional stability, optimism, self-esteem, planning ahead, positivity

GREEN: Peace of mind, balance, love, sympathy, harmony, adaptability

BLUE: Ability to think logically, self-expression, retentive memory, focus

VIOLET: Higher mind, spirituality, connection with the Universal Life Force

The final step is to create an affirmation that relates to your specific goal. An affirmation is a short positive saying that you repeat to yourself over and over again until your mind accepts it, and it becomes a natural part of your life. Affirmations are always said in the present tense, as if you already possess the desired quality. If your goal is to increase your self-esteem, you might say: "I feel good about myself," or "I am a worthwhile, lovable person." If you suffer from lack of motivation, you might say: "I have plenty of enthusiasm and energy."

Finally, once you've done all this, you can imprint the qualities you desire into your aura. Here are the steps to do this:

1. Relax quietly in the usual way.

2. Once you feel totally relaxed, think about the first item on your list. Imagine a scene in which you are demonstrating this

quality. Hold on to this image for as long as possible. Alternatively, you might visualize yourself chatting with someone you respect and admire. This person is telling you that one of the things he really likes about you is the fact that you possess this particular quality, and use it well.

3. Visualize yourself, and picture your aura surrounding you. Allow the aura to expand to at least twice its normal size.

4. Take seven slow, deep breaths. Each time you inhale, imagine that you're breathing in the color that you've associated with the quality you are imprinting in your aura. Each time you exhale, visualize that color spreading out and into every part of your aura. By the time you've exhaled seven times, this color will be visible in every part of your aura.

5. Visualize a sign hanging above your head. On this sign are written words that describe the quality you are seeking. Reach up and take hold of the sign. Place it inside your aura, and watch as it duplicates itself over and over again, until your aura appears to consist of nothing except your chosen color and hundreds of signs. Hold this image for as long as possible.

6. Tell yourself that the quality or trait you desire is now imprinted into every part of your aura, as well as your physical body, and you now possess an abundance of this quality. Smile, and enjoy the feeling of knowing that every cell of your body now possesses the desired quality, and that you'll never lack it again.

7. Repeat Step 2.

8. Congratulate yourself on gaining a valuable quality that will help you achieve your dreams.

9. Silently repeat the affirmation you created several times, using as much emotion as possible.

10. Take three slow, deep breaths, and become familiar with the room you are in. Lie quietly for a minute or two before opening your eyes. When you feel ready, get up, have something to eat or drnk, and carry on with your day.

The exercise is now complete, but you now need to put yourself into a situation where you can demonstrate the quality you have imprinted into your being. If, for instance, you were asking for motivation, immediately get busy and start work on a project that you'd put off in the past. If you asked for more confidence, deliberately place yourself in a situation that you would have avoided, or found difficult, in the past.

If the results are not as good as you would like, repeat the exercise as many times as necessary until you achieve success. Once the first item on the list has been achieved, repeat this exercise with the second item, and continue in this way until you have achieved all of them. Then, of course, it's time to make another list.

You can use this exercise for other forms of self-improvement, too. If, for instance, you want to lose weight, you could start by visualizing yourself the size, shape, and weight you want to be. Picture that as clearly as possible for as long as you can. Create an affirmation for yourself. It might be: "I eat just enough food to keep me healthy, fit, and happy," or "I enjoy life, and enjoy food in moderation." As people eat for many different reasons, it might be hard to find the right color from the list above. If you are an emotional eater, you might choose yellow. If you eat too much when you're stressed, you might choose green or blue. If you're not sure, use a pure white light. Imprint your goal into the white light, and repeat regularly until you reach your goal weight.

I have worked with a large number of overweight people over the years. Most of them are looking for a quick and easy answer to their problem. Losing weight takes time and effort. Doing this exercise will help, but will not work without input from you. If you're serious about losing weight, you'll also need to exercise and may need to change your eating and drinking habits.

HOW TO NURTURE A TALENT

Everyone has a talent or gift that they were given at birth. I constantly meet people who tell me they don't have a talent, but this isn't true. People say, "I wish I could sing," or "I wish I could paint." Maybe they can't do those things, but you can guarantee they possess a skill of some sort.

A young lady I know has an incredible ability at getting along with absolutely everyone. She doesn't consider this a talent, but it most certainly is, and she's using it to great effect in her career.

A few years ago, we employed a man to do some landscaping work in our garden. He gave us some excellent ideas and did a wonderful job for us. He has a talent for this sort of work.

A young mother we know has started a small catering business at home. She started by producing children's birthday cakes, and now she caters for children's birthday parties. She's turned her talent into a business that's helping support her family.

Everyone is creative in his or her own way. You don't have to be a great singer or artist to be creative. The mother who bakes cakes is doing creative work, as is the landscape gardener we employed.

People who are making use of their talent are usually happy. This is because they're doing something that they're naturally good at, and because of this, they enjoy doing it. They're also better at it than people who don't share the same talent.

If you feel that you don't have a talent, ask your friends and family. They'll be happy to tell you what you're good at. You may find that you have several talents that you were unaware of until your friends told you about them.

Once you've found your talent, you need to nurture it. You may need to take classes or courses to develop your skills. You may need to do whatever it is over and over again until you've honed those skills. You should also spend time with people who have the same, or a similar, talent. I know two people who are good friends. One is a portrait artist, and the other is a caricaturist. They've both learned from each other, even though their specific talents are different.

You'll find that when you're working on your talent, your aura will expand, reflecting the joy you're experiencing as you work. You can enhance this by breathing in a color that relates to your talent. The landscape gardener, for instance, might choose to breathe in green, as it reflects his work environment. A teacher might breathe in yellow, as his or her work involves mental effort. The lady who caters for children's parties might breathe in red, as she's working in her own business.

At times you might have doubts about your talent. If this occurs, seal your aura from negativity, and cleanse and balance your aura.

People who use their talents in their careers invariably do well, as work becomes a form of play. These people are anything but average, and their growth and development is a joy to behold.

The ability to see and interpret auras is a significant talent that you'll be able to use to help yourself and others. As your skills develop, you'll find you can read the auras of animals, also. How to do this is the subject of the next chapter.

11

THE AURAS OF PETS

MANY YEARS AGO, I received a phone call from someone who had attended a course I'd given on aura reading. She was so excited that for several seconds she could hardly speak.

"I came home tonight, and my cat was at the door to greet me, just as she always is," she finally managed to tell me. "But tonight I saw a glowing aura all around her!"

I started to congratulate her, when she interrupted.

"Is it good that I can see her aura? It doesn't mean she's not going to be all right, does it?"

I assured her that it was good news that she could see her cat's aura, and that she had probably seen it because she had recently gained aura awareness, and her cat's aura had expanded as she was pleased to see her mistress back home again.

"I can still see it now," she told me. "But will I be able to see it tomorrow?"

"Yes, of course. You'll be able to help your pet so much more now that you can see her aura."

I've had many similar conversations over the years, including many with people who have learned to see auras around people, but were surprised to discover their pets also had auras that can be seen and interpreted.

Sometimes people ask me why I'd want to look at a pet's aura. I always reply that I want my pets to be happy, and this is revealed in their auras. Even more important is the fact that health indications can be seen in the aura, which means I can seek veterinary help when any potential illness is still at an early stage.

Conversely, I've also met keen gardeners who could see auras around their plants, and were surprised to discover that they themselves possessed auras.

If you have done all the exercises in this book, you'll have no difficulty in seeing your pets' auras. Most of the time, the auras of animals are more subdued and not as gloriously radiant as human auras, but the different layers and colors can be clearly discerned.

There are two ways to start looking at the auras of animals. If your pet is a cat or dog, you can play with it for several minutes first. This causes the aura to expand, making it easier to see. Once you have finished the game, stand or sit several feet away from your pet, and focus on something a few feet beyond his or her head. You will notice a grayish aura surrounding your pet. Initially, the color of your pet's coat will affect your ability to see the colors in his or her aura. Despite this, it won't take long before you start to see the colors in your pet's aura. If you have not practiced the earlier exercises with people, you may start by seeing your pet's etheric double, and gradually become aware of the different layers in his or her aura.

The other method is to simply gaze beyond your pet while he or she is sitting still. This method is not as easy initially, as the aura is partly obscured by your pet's fur. However, it is often a more practical way to do the exercise. While the playtime in the first method expands the aura, very often your pet will want to continue the game you instigated and will not sit quietly long enough.

Once you are able to see the aura surrounding your pet, you will start noticing the auras of other animals. This can be useful. If, for example, you see ugly colors in the aura of a dog that appears to be sitting or lying down placidly, you'll know that you shouldn't approach the animal.

The colors you see in your pet's aura do not have the same meanings as those found in humans. This is because animals do not possess the same level of consciousness that we do. However, some colors are easy to interpret. Dark red, for instance, indicates anger and a bad temper. Light blue indicates a peaceful, placid temperament. Yellow is a sign of shrewdness, slyness, and cunning. Green indicates an animal who is a creature of habit, and needs a regular routine.

THE CHAKRAS

Animals have the same seven main chakras that humans do, and they are situated in much the same position as ours along their spinal column. The root chakra, for instance, is found at the base of the tail and the crown chakra is on top of the head.

In addition to this, animals have an important additional chakra called the brachial chakra.[1] This chakra is at the top of the animal's shoulders, and can be felt on either side of his or her body. This chakra is the most powerful energy center in the animal's body, as it activates all the other chakras. It is also the most important one as far as interaction between animals and humans is concerned.

Root Chakra

POSITION: At the base of the tail where it meets the body
COLOR: Red
ELEMENT: Earth
GEMSTONE: Red jasper, garnet

The root chakra relates to grounding and the survival instinct. When it is out of balance, the animal will be fearful, anxious, restless, and possibly underweight. He or she will also demonstrate unusually strong fight or flight characteristics.

The root chakra looks after the intestines, the hind legs, hips, and the skeletal system.

Sacral Chakra

POSITION: Between the tail and the middle of the back

COLOR: Orange

ELEMENT: Water

GEMSTONE: Orange calcite, carnelian

The sacral chakra is concerned with emotions and sexuality. Obviously, this chakra is strongly affected when the animal is neutered or castrated. When this chakra is out of balance, the animal will be overly emotional and may whine for no apparent reason.

The sacral chakra looks after the kidneys, adrenal glands, and the reproductive and lymphatic systems.

Solar Plexus Chakra

POSITION: Middle of the back

COLOR: Yellow

ELEMENT: Fire

GEMSTONE: Tiger's eye, topaz

The solar plexus chakra is concerned with the animal's sense of personal power. This chakra relates to self-awareness in non-domesticated animals. When this chakra is out of balance, the animal will be withdrawn and unresponsive. He or she may also be overly aggressive.

The solar plexus chakra looks after the stomach, liver, and digestive tract.

Heart Chakra

POSITION: The breast, in the area between the front of the chest
and on the back behind the front legs

COLOR: Green

ELEMENT: Air

GEMSTONE: Emerald, green jade

The heart chakra is concerned with relationships, especially those related to the hierarchy of the group. When this chakra is out of balance, the animal will be nervous, jealous, withdrawn, and overly possessive.

The heart chakra relates to the heart and lungs, as well as the immune system.

Throat Chakra

POSITION: In the throat area of the neck

COLOR: Blue

GEMSTONE: All blue stones, including lace agate, quartz, and topaz

The throat chakra is concerned with communication, both with other animals of his or her species, and also humans (with domesticated animals). When this chakra is out of balance, the animal will react in one of two ways: he or she will be extremely uncommunicative or alternatively, extremely noisy.

The throat chakra relates to the throat, teeth, and jaws.

Brow Chakra

POSITION: Just above the eyes

COLOR: Indigo

GEMSTONE: Lapis lazuli, amethyst

The brow chakra is concerned with self-acceptance. When this chakra is out of balance, the animal will seem distant and unresponsive.

The brow chakra relates to the pineal gland and the head.

Crown Chakra

POSITION: Between the ears, on top of the head
COLOR: Violet
GEMSTONE: Diamond, clear quartz

The crown chakra enables the animal to connect with the Universal Life Force. When this chakra is out of balance, the animal will appear withdrawn, and will lack the will to live.

The crown chakra relates to the brain, pituitary gland, and the animal's skin.

Brachial Chakra

POSITION: At the top of the shoulders
COLOR: All colors
GEMSTONE: Clear quartz, black tourmaline

The brachial chakra connects the seven other major chakras. It is concerned with the bond that can develop between the animal and humans. It is the animal's major chakra, and is the first chakra that should be utilized when doing any form of aura or chakra healing. When this chakra is out of balance, the animal will avoid being touched, and will refuse to relate to people.

The brachial chakra relates to the chest, neck, and the forelegs.

Bud Chakras

Animals also possess bud chakras, which are minor energy centers, on each paw and at the entrance to each ear. The bud chakras are highly sensitive and enable animals to feel vibrations through their paws. These bud chakras explain why animals frequently paw the ground before lying down. Bud chakras may also help animals ground themselves to the earth.

CHAKRA HEALING

If your pet is unwell, you can aid the healing process by working with his or her chakras. You can do this either by stimulating the energy fields, or with physical contact. When working with animals, I prefer the latter. Start by working with his or her brachial chakra, and follow this by energizing the root chakra. Work your way along his or her back and finish with the crown chakra. If you wish, you can include the bud chakras as part of the therapy. Talk to your pet in a conversational tone while working on his or her chakras. You'll find your pet will thoroughly enjoy these sessions, and in addition to the healing benefits, you'll find the bond you and your pet share will strengthen.

Any form of chakra healing should be done as an adjunct to traditional therapy. If your pet is in pain or is noticeably unwell, you must take him or her to your veterinarian. Keep your chakra healing sessions short to begin with, and gradually lengthen them as your pet becomes used to them.

If working with animals in this way appeals to you, you'll find plenty of opportunities to practice. All you need do is tell people of your interest, and they'll be keen for you to have a look at their pet. You'll be able to help many animals, and their owners, by doing this.

You can develop your skills at reading animals' auras everywhere you go. A visit to the zoo, or a trip to the country, becomes much more fascinating when you pause to look at the auras of the different animals you see.

Many people become psychic readers because they have a talent for helping others, animals as well as people. The ability to encourage, help, motivate, and inspire others helps them grow as well. Even if you have no desire to become an aura reader, you'll find it interesting to read the next chapter and learn how it is done.

12

HOW TO GIVE AURA READINGS

AS YOUR ABILITY to sense and see auras develops, people will start asking you about their auras. Most will want to know what colors you can see. Once you've told them, they'll ask what the colors mean. In time, you might want to develop this ability and start giving readings.

You can help many people by doing this. Most people go through life unaware of the talents and skills they possess. Even if they are aware of a latent ability, they may not choose to develop it unless they receive encouragement. As an aura reader, this is something you can do. I've seen many people start to develop their skills after being encouraged to do so during a psychic reading. One of the most satisfying aspects of aura reading is the many opportunities it provides to motivate people to achieve their dreams.

Your readings should be positive and motivating. Naturally, you'll see many negative auras. This gives you an opportunity to advise the person to change his or her way of thinking, which will, if accepted and followed, lead to a more fulfilling and happy life.

You should never give medical advice when giving aura readings. In fact, unless you have medical qualifications, it's illegal. Medical intuitives perform valuable work by examining people's auric fields, but this is never done in the course of a general reading.

You need special qualities to become an aura reader. Obviously, you must be able to see auras. In addition, you need to be kind, gentle, empathetic, and understanding. You must have a desire to help others. People are extremely vulnerable when they come for a reading. You'll see good and bad things in most people's auras. You need to focus on the positive, but also deal gently and sympathetically with your clients' negative qualities.

You need to keep everything you learn during a reading confidential. Your clients will confide in you, and they have a right to expect everything they say to remain a secret between the two of you. A gossip would not last long as a psychic reader.

Giving a reading is not an excuse for an ego trip. In fact, the reader's ego should be almost invisible. The purpose of a reading is to help and educate the person being read, rather than to bolster your self-esteem.

To give good readings, you need to be mentally and spiritually prepared.

ADVANCE PREPARATION

It's important that your mind is relaxed. You can't give good readings if your mind is mulling over your own problems. Mental preparation comes in various forms. Some people like to meditate. Others like to sit in a relaxing environment and listen to music. Some people enjoy lighting candles and burning incense. Many readers pray before giving a reading. I take several slow, deep breaths, as these help me enter the desired state of mind. By doing these things, readers separate themselves from their everyday lives, and are able to focus entirely on the concerns of their clients.

You should also remind yourself about how privileged you are to be able to help people by giving them a reading. I always approach a reading seriously, but also maintain a sense of fun and expectation. I try to be relaxed, yet alert and aware.

Do not attempt aura readings if you're feeling exhausted. When you're tired you'll miss many of the subtle nuances of information that are essential to an effective reading. This is not fair to the person you are reading for.

PSYCHIC PROTECTION

It makes good sense to protect yourself while giving readings. Some of your clients will arrive with negative thoughts and emotions, and you don't want to absorb any of them.

The simplest way to protect yourself is to imagine yourself surrounded by a pure white protective light. Visualize this white light descending from above, entering your body through your crown chakra, and surrounding your body with strength, love, and protection.

If you have a special room that you use for your readings, imagine it filled with white light, too.

ESSENTIAL REQUIREMENTS

Fortunately, you do not need much in the way of equipment to give aura readings. All you need are drawing implements and paper. I have an outline of a slightly androgynous looking person that I photocopy onto sheets of good-quality paper. I copy one hundred at a time, add a sheet of thick cardboard at the back, and glue them at one narrow end to create a pad. If you can draw an outline of the person you are reading for, you are fortunate because you can buy artists pads, and use them. I've met several aura readers who are also good artists, and I envy their ability to draw both the person, and his or her aura. However, I shouldn't worry, as no one has ever complained about the aura portraits I produce.

I also have a set of colored pencils. I use Cumberland Derwent artists' pencils. These are quality pencils, and the set includes indigo, a color that is sometimes hard to find. Some people prefer to use colored markers, but I started with pencils and have been happy with them. You should experiment until you find the right pens, pencils, crayons, or markers for you. It's easy enough to find suitable implements, but it can be difficult to find them with all the colors you need.

GIVING THE READING

Spend a few minutes chatting with your client before starting the reading. This helps your client to relax and make some decisions about you, if he or she hasn't met you before. Likewise, you'll make a number of assumptions about your client, too.

Once your client is relaxed, explain briefly what you're going to do. Every reader has his or her own way of conducting a reading. I like to start by feeling the aura. After this, I sit down and draw the aura while talking about what I see and what it means. As I'm not an artist, I draw the aura colors around the pre-drawn outline of an androgynous looking person.

This has worked extremely well for me over the years, and no one has ever commented on the generic outline. I've visited many homes over the years, and found my artwork framed and hanging on the wall. Although what I do is acceptable, I wish I had more artistic ability. It would be wonderful to quickly sketch a likeness of the person before discussing the aura. However, the most important part of the session is the actual reading, rather than the aura portrait. You need not be concerned about lack of artistic ability if you intend becoming an aura reader.

I have comfortable chairs in my office, and we sit down in those for the first few minutes. After I've explained the procedure, I move the client to a straight-backed, office-type chair, which is about six feet away from a plain white wall. This setup provides a good background, which makes it easy for me to see the aura, and allows me to move freely around the client while feeling his or her aura.

I have a similar chair that I sit on while drawing the aura. This is about six feet away from the client, and all the main lighting in the room is behind me.

The last thing I do before starting the reading is to briefly hold hands with the client. I hold my palms out, facing up, with my fingers slightly separated and ask the client to place his or her palms face down on mine. This helps me to tune in to the energy of the person I'm reading for. Many clients say they experience a tingling feeling when we hold our palms together. While our palms are still touching, I close my eyes momentarily, and give thanks for the opportunity of being able to help the person I'm reading for.

Usually, it's an extremely positive feeling to hold hands in this way. Occasionally you'll experience an unpleasant, uncomfortable sensation. When this occurs, I move my hands away after a few seconds, then discreetly touch a wooden surface to allow the negativity to flow out of my fingertips and into the wood.

SAMPLE READING

Here's an example of a typical reading that I gave a thirty-year-old woman called Alice. I'll start at the point where she is sitting in the chair facing me. I hold my hands out, palms up.

"Would you please place your palms on mine," I say. "This helps me tune in to your energies. That's very good. You have a strong vibration." I close my eyes briefly and give thanks for the opportunity to help her as much as I can.

When we separate our hands, I smile at her. "I'm going to start by feeling your aura, and then I'll draw it while explaining it all to you. You may sense my hands contacting your aura while I'm feeling it. If you close your eyes, you'll be more likely to notice it."

Most people close their eyes, but some feel uncomfortable doing this while a stranger is walking around them feeling their aura. I feel the aura using the methods we discussed in chapter 2. As Alice has her eyes closed, I tell her where I am and what I'm doing at each stage. I finish this part by feeling her chakras.

"Good. You survived that," I say. "Did you feel my hands touching your aura?"

Most people respond positively to this question, especially if they followed my suggestion and closed their eyes. Many people feel a sensation when my hands are close to one or two of their chakras, even if they don't notice anything else.

"I did in a few places," Alice says. She indicates her stomach, chest, and the top of her head.

"That's good. There's a reason why you felt my hands in those places, and I'll tell you about that later."

I keep my artist's pad and colored pencils on my desk. I pick up the pad, and start looking at her aura. I am already aware of her main colors, of course, as she's been in my office for more than ten minutes. However, I haven't told her anything about her colors yet. I study her aura for about thirty seconds before reaching over to pick up the first colored pencil. As Alice's ground color is yellow, I pick up a yellow pencil.

"I see a great deal of yellow about you," I say. I start drawing a large band of yellow around the outline of the preprinted figure on my pad of paper. As I'm right-handed, I draw the right-hand side of the aura first. Once I've finished it, I show it to Alice.

"This wide band of yellow is the start of your aura, Alice. You'll notice that it starts about an eighth of an inch away from the outline. That doesn't mean your aura starts somewhere outside your body. In fact, it's an emanation of every cell in your body. The area closest to your skin is called the etheric double. It's virtually colorless, with a fine gray tinge to it, and that's why I haven't tried to draw it. It constantly moves and shimmers. It's a fascinating part of the aura, as it expands when you're asleep and contracts when you're awake. Some people think that because of this, it's a sort of battery that recharges itself overnight. Your etheric double is beautiful and clear. This is a sign of good health. It also shows you think positively, most of the time. People who constantly look on the negative side of everything tend to have rather murky-looking etheric doubles."

I lean back in my chair and continue drawing the left-hand side of Alice's aura. I continue talking while doing this.

"The yellow in your aura is sometimes known as your ground color. This color is important, as it shows what you should be doing with your life. It doesn't mean it's what you're actually doing, of course. However, if you are, you'll feel incredibly fulfilled, as you'll be doing what you are meant to be doing in this incarnation.

"You'll always be a fun person to be with, as your ground color is yellow. It relates to enthusiasm and quick thinking. You'd be hard to keep up with at times! You enjoy people, and love entertaining and being entertained. You have an excellent brain, and anything that interests you, you learn quickly. However, your quick mind can sometimes be your enemy, as you might be inclined to dabble in many fields, rather than focus all your energies and talents on just one. You're highly creative, but again you probably don't know which of several options you should pursue."

Alice smiles. "That sounds like me."

"Ideally, you should be using your many talents, including your people skills, your significant verbal ability, your good taste, your creativity, and your good brain in some area that provides you with enough stimulation and satisfaction. You need to express yourself in some sort of way, ideally creatively."

"I sort of know that," Alice comments, "But I haven't managed to find it yet."

"I might have a few suggestions by the time we've finished," I say. It's extremely common for people to have a vague idea about what they should be doing with their lives, but struggle to find a way to harness it. I also find people who already know what they should be doing, but hold themselves back from doing it. Fear, doubt, and worry play a part in this, of course. It's easier to stay in a safe, secure job than it is to take a risk that could end in failure. Thoreau said these people 'lead lives of quiet desperation.'"

By this time, I've finished drawing Alice's ground color. I turn it around to show her.

"Yellow is the most important color in your aura," I continue. "However, most people also have colors that radiate outward through the aura. Some people have none; others one or two, and a few have the whole rainbow. You have three radiating colors."

I reach for a red pencil, and hold it up to let Alice see it.

"The most visible of these in your aura is red."

In Alice's case, the red is mainly around her head and neck. I quickly draw a series of red lines radiating through the aura, and show it to Alice while I talk about it.

"Red is a powerful color. It gives you drive and energy. It shows you like to be the person in charge. You naturally assume responsibility, no matter what situation you find yourself within. You have your own special, original, and progressive approach to everything you do, and you don't need much input from others. Red shows you should aim high. If you aim low, you'll achieve it, but you'll never be fully satisfied. If you aim high, you'll probably reach your goal, but it will probably take longer than you'd like. This is because your yellow ground color finds it hard to remain focused on one goal for any length of time. However, the creativity and intellect of the yellow, coupled with the drive and ambition of the red, make a powerful combination."

I pause to see if Alice has anything to say about this.

"I always feel good when I wear red," she says. "Is this because it's in my aura?"

I nod my head. "That's right. You're likely to enjoy wearing clothes that include yellow and your radiating colors. As a bonus, people will always say these colors suit you. Although they may not be able to see your aura, they'll sense that these are 'your' colors."

"Red makes me feel confident, too."

"That's right. I sometimes suggest people wear a bit of red if they need to feel confident in a potentially difficult situation. In your case, it's even better, as people will also say red suits you."

I replace the red pencil, and check Alice's aura again before picking up a green pencil.

"Your second most important radiating color is green. Interestingly, most of the green appears in your chest area. It's interesting, as your heart chakra, in your chest, is green. However, this is not coming from the chakra. It's a radiating color."

I draw the green radiating colors. There are some in the head area, a few radiate from her legs, but by far the majority radiate from her chest. Again, I show the aura portrait to her.

"Green is an interesting color. It's a healing color, which means you'd make a very good natural healer. However, especially looked at in conjunction with the yellow and red we already have, it's a useful addition to your set of skills. It shows you enjoy a challenge. Despite the skimming-over-the-surface tendencies of your ground color, when you find a worthwhile goal or project, you're prepared to work as long and as hard as necessary to achieve it. It gives you perseverance, determination, and a sense of responsibility. Green also gives you the ability to organize and manage others. It's a strong and powerful color."

Alice frowns. "I don't see myself as a healer. I must admit, I dabbled with aromatherapy and massage, but they were short-term interests."

"That means they satisfied your yellow ground color, but weren't the right healing modality to satisfy your yellow and red. Probably, for you, the more important aspect of the green is that it gives you drive and persistence."

"If there's something I really want."

I nod, and look at her aura again. "Okay, your final radiating color is blue."

"I love blue! I'm wearing blue today!"

Her blue radiating color seems to be evenly spaced around Alice's aura. I quickly draw them in, and again let Alice see the result.

"Okay. What does the blue mean?"

"It's a good color, and one that harmonizes well with your other main colors. It shows that you need a great deal of freedom and variety in your life. You're talented and versatile, and good at coming up with interesting ideas. You can present your ideas well, too. You'd probably enjoy travel. You're unlikely to find a standard nine-to-five job satisfying for any length of time, as no job can provide the excitement and adventure you crave.

"Let me briefly explain how blue gets on well with your other main colors. Yellow and blue go together well, as the yellow comes up with great ideas that the blue acts upon. The creative aspects of the yellow are enhanced by the variety and stimulating lifestyle promised by the blue.

"Most of the time, blue also gets on well with red. Red needs a challenge, and all the exciting opportunities blue provides help red find interesting and often unusual areas to explore. However, the ambition of red is sometimes lost because the blue pulls in so many different directions. Blue and green don't always get along. Green wants to follow something through, all the way to completion, but blue seeks freedom and variety. However, if blue can provide the right opportunity, the green will be able to follow it through to completion."

"You've lost me. Can you go through that again?"

I explain the combinations of colors again before continuing.

"For you to be happy and fulfilled, you need to somehow satisfy the needs and desires of all four colors. The yellow, as it's your ground color, is by far the most important. For most people, balancing their colors is something of a juggling act. In your case, it's not quite so difficult, as most of the time they harmonize well with each other."

"That's interesting," Alice says. She smiles, and says, "You said you might have some suggestions for me."

"That's right. I think you've come to see me at a good time, as you're only now starting to think about the life you want to lead in the future. In some ways, you're maturing late. I personally think that's wonderful, as you've enjoyed doing so many different things over the years. You've made lots of friends, experimented with different forms of creativity, and learned a little bit about almost everything. This all comes from your ground color. Now, you've come to the realization that you want more from your life than endless fun and frivolity."

"Yes, but I still want fun in the future."

"You'll always have fun, no matter what you do. Yellow is essentially fun-loving, after all. Now, for the future, you need to harness the talents yellow has endowed you with, and use the other colors to help you make productive use of them."

"Such as?"

"Well, yellow gives you a talent with words. You could speak or write, for instance. Teaching and acting would have you in front of people expressing yourself. You could do well in selling or entertaining. Your talent with words probably extends to writing, too. With your interest in travel, maybe you could become a travel writer.

"You'd probably do extremely well in business, and that might be a good way for you to get the variety you need. You'd get great satisfaction from dealing with items you found attractive. You could use your good taste to buy beautiful objects to sell. You also have considerable people skills, so a business such as conference organizing or an entertainment agency might appeal. Whatever it is, it must involve regular contact with others. The red and green give you the necessary ambition and persistence to succeed at any business that appealed to you. Self-employment would be an excellent way to use all of your main colors.

"Working for others, you'd need plenty of room around you in which to work. You'd need continued opportunities to grow and develop, and you'd have to use your communication skills in some way. You need a degree of freedom, and always work best when you know what the job is, and you're left to get on with it."

Alice smiles. "That gives me a lot to think about."

"What sort of work are you doing now?"

"I'm PA for the CEO of a large retail chain."

"Do you enjoy it?"

"It's funny you should ask that. I used to. It gives me variety and people contact, which, as you know, I need. But I've been doing it for three years now, and it's no longer fun. I can do it with my eyes closed. My boss is a nice man. He's kind and generous, and I like working for him. But it's time for me to find something more challenging."

"Is that why you came for a reading?"

Alice laughs. "It's something that's always fascinated me. I see colors around people occasionally, but I don't know what they mean. It's something I'll go into one day."

"Are you looking for another job?"

"No. I'm hoping to set up my own business. When I was in Italy last year I bought a beautiful mosaic picture, and some miniatures. They're all copies of famous art works, and the prices were good. My friends love them, and I think I could turn them into a business. I'll bring in a few, sell them, and then do it again and again, until I have enough money to do it full time."

I nod enthusiastically. "That sounds like a good plan. When are you going to start?"

"Today! I wanted to hear what you had to say first, and everything you said made me think my idea would work. Thank you!"

"That's my pleasure. What you're planning sounds perfect for you. Now we're not quite finished. I need to add your chakras. Usually, I don't see them, but gain a sense of them. Also, of course, I felt them at the start. I draw them as little rosebuds, and as you'll see, they follow the colors of the rainbow."

I stop speaking while drawing the chakras. As I sensed more activity in her crown chakra, I draw that with a trace of a spiral heading upward. After doing this, I again show her what I've done.

"The chakras are energy centers inside the aura. Yours are well-balanced and vibrant. You mentioned sensing my hands in three places when I was feeling your aura. These were at your solar plexus, heart, and crown chakra positions. Because there was more energy in the crown chakra, I added this smoke-like energy emanating from it. It's fairly unusual for someone to have a particularly strong crown chakra. Are you working on the spiritual side of your nature?"

"I'm trying to. I don't go to church, but I meditate every day, and I have a small altar at home. It's something I can't really explain. I have a fascination with the spiritual side of life."

"You should carry on doing what you're already doing," I said. "As the results are clearly in your aura."

I sign and date the aura portrait, and give it to Alice. "I feel embarrassed giving my artwork to someone who obviously appreciates beautiful things, but I hope you'll enjoy looking at this every now and again as you start your new venture. Do you have any questions?"

"No, I don't. You've covered pretty much everything I was concerned about. Oh, one thing. Will I ever settle down?"

"Yes, you will, but you're not ready yet. You need a very special partner, someone who'll give you the freedom you need to learn and grow all the way through life. I'd concentrate on your new business first, and get that up and running. Once you've done that, I think you'll find the right person without much effort. You're sociable and get on well with people. People like having you around. Your problem is likely to be choosing one person out of many."

"Thanks, and thank you for the reading."

Most people ask questions at the end of a reading. Often, the questions are the most important things on their mind, and they have to be covered in depth. Alice's main concern was her career, and where to go from here. Her question about settling down wasn't a great concern, and I was able to deal with it briefly.

That's an example of a fairly typical aura reading. As a general rule, people don't go to aura readers for the same reasons they go to a fortune-teller. They want to know more about themselves and their talents and potentials. Aura reading is extremely useful for this, and once you start doing them, your popularity will increase enormously.

BRIEF AURA READINGS

Your aura readings need not necessarily be in-depth. In fact, when you're starting out, you should keep them brief, and gradually extend them as you gain experience.

Fortunately, you can do brief aura readings wherever you go. It's easy to find people who'd like to have their auras drawn for them. All you need do is mention that you're studying the subject, and people will want to know more.

I frequently do brief aura readings on the back of my business card. I draw a simple stick figure, surround it with the ground color, and add the radiating colors. If I don't have my colored pencils with me, I do the whole thing with a ballpoint pen, and write in the colors I see.

I also sometimes do aura readings in a party or group situation. In this case, the readings need to be very brief (no longer than five minutes), and usually I have a line of people waiting for their turn. These readings also attract a crowd of interested people who try to see the aura of the person I am reading for. Often, they do. Naturally, as I'm being paid for my services, in this type of situation I use my colored pencils and a half-sized pad with the preprinted figure on it. I use the smaller pads for quick readings as it takes less time to draw the aura around a small figure.

Interestingly, in a group situation I read for almost as many men as I do women. There's a misconception that women are interested in these things, but men aren't. I find that men are initially hesitant, and this is possibly because they don't want their male colleagues to make fun of them. However, once their wives or partners have had a reading, they'll insist that he does, too. Once one man has been brave enough to have a reading, many more will follow.

Here's an example of a brief reading. There's no time to relax the person, ask questions, or feel the aura. The person may have been waiting in line for a while, and will be happy to sit down. In this type of situation, the person sits four or five feet away from me. I have a soft light source behind me that focuses on the floor between us. As well as making it easier for me to see the person's aura, it also creates a "circle of intimacy," even in a crowded room.

I reach over and shake the person's hand.

"Hi, I'm Richard," I say. "What's your name?"

"John."

"Hi, John." I lean back in my chair and look at his aura. Most of the time I'll already know his colors because I saw them while he was waiting in line. However, a bit of window-dressing helps in an entertainment situation, and I can't make it look too easy. My pencils are on a small table to my right. I move my right hand to and fro over them, and pick up the color that relates to his ground color.

"Your main color, John, is green." I draw a wide band of green around the figure as I talk. "Green is a powerful, practical color. It shows you're a good organizer, you're extremely conscientious, and you're good with details. You're responsible, and take your work seriously. You'd make an excellent manager. You have plenty of stamina and energy, and are prepared to work long and hard when necessary. You may not see it in yourself, but there is a stubborn side to your nature. Once you've made your mind up on something, it's extremely hard to change it."

By this time, I've finished the ground color, and I look at John's aura again to confirm his radiating colors. I pick up the indigo pencil and show it to him.

"Are you familiar with the color indigo?"

Most people say, "no," but a few say, "isn't that the color of the sea?"

"It's in between blue and violet." I draw in the radiating color as I speak. "You have quite a bit of indigo radiating from your head and shoulders. This color relates very much to home and family. You'll always be happiest in that type of situation. You're loving, kind and caring. You'd make a wonderful father. You're probably the person in the family people go to when they're having problems in their lives, as they can confide in you."

I replace the indigo pencil, and appear to hesitate before picking up the orange pencil.

"There's also a trace of orange in your aura. This shows that you'll always be close to the important people in your life. You're considerate and sensitive to the feelings of others. All your close relationships will continue to grow and develop all the way through your life. You're a very fortunate person."

I remove the sheet from the pad, and hand it to him. This tells him the reading is over. Usually, at this stage, the person gets up and the next person in line sits down. Every now and again, someone will ask a question. When this occurs, I answer it as quickly as possible. If I cannot answer it in sixty seconds, I'll ask the person to contact me privately. In this case, I'd give him or her my business card. When I stopped doing private readings, I started handing out the card of an aura reader I trusted, and told people to contact her.

I find it both stimulating and exhausting to give dozens of quick readings in a row. I take a sip of water between each person. Nowadays, I also stop for five minutes every hour. This allows me to stand up, stretch, and take several deep breaths, so that I'm recharged and ready to start again. Although it can be hard work at times, they're great fun to do. It's also a good way to examine a large number of auras in a short period of time.

Aura reading is not for everyone. However, if you enjoy it, you'll find many opportunities to practice.

OTHER TYPES OF READINGS

A number of psychic readers use the aura in their readings, even though their main emphasis is on, say, the Tarot or numerology. Numerology uses numbers to determine character and make predictions about the future. Each color of the aura is related to a number:

1 = Red	5 = Blue	9 = Bronze
2 = Orange	6 = Indigo	11 = Silver
3 = Yellow	7 = Violet	22 = Gold
4 = Green	8 = Pink	

In numerology, each number is reduced to a single digit with the exception of the two Master numbers, 11 and 22. The presence of a Master number is an indication of an old soul, someone who has lived many times before.

If a numerologist saw red in someone's aura, he or she would interpret that as a 1 numerologically. Likewise, blue would be interpreted as a 5.

Tarot card readers sometimes do chakra readings with their cards. They deal out seven cards to represent the different chakras. The first card dealt relates to the root chakra, the second to the sacral, and so on. The cards are interpreted by relating the meaning of each card with the energies of the particular chakra. Consequently, the first card dealt would be interpreted in light of the sense of stability and security provided by the root chakra. The fourth card dealt relates to the peace, joy, and love of the heart chakra, and is interpreted with that in mind.

Psychic readers frequently use two or three different modalities in their readings. People like the fact that they can have, say, a palmistry reading, but also learn something about their auras, numbers, or Tarot cards at the same time.

CONCLUSION

CONGRATULATIONS ON GETTING this far. By now you'll know how useful and practical the ability to see auras can be, and I hope you're using this knowledge to help yourself, family, and friends. You'll find the more you learn about auras, the more there is to learn. It's a fascinating subject, with many possible uses.

Not long ago, a friend of my younger son told me how practical the ability to read auras was for him. He'd become heavily involved in gambling and was playing poker for high stakes. One evening, he told me, he looked at the auras of the people he was playing with, and discovered they were all "murky, with horrible colors." He realized that these people were cardsharps who were probably cheating him at cards. He told them he had a headache, and stopped playing. He never went back.

It's useful to be able to determine someone's honesty and intentions, but as you now know, your newfound skill will help you in many other ways, as well.

Please read this book again, and spend as much time as necessary to master the different exercises. Once you've become familiar with everything in this book, you should read as many other books on the subject as possible. You'll find many different points of view on the subject. This is as it should be, as everyone sees auras in their own special way.

I hope the information in this book will help you achieve your goals, and gain confidence and vibrant health. I also hope it will help you develop psychically and spiritually. I wish you great success in your quest.

SUGGESTED READING

Andrews, Ted. *How to Heal with Color*. St. Paul, MN: Llewellyn Publications, 1992.

———. *How to See and Read the Aura*. St. Paul, MN: Llewellyn Publications, 1991.

Bacci, Ingrid. *The Art of Effortless Living: Simple Techniques for Healing Mind, Body and Spirit*. New York: Vision Works Publishing, 2000.

Baker, Dr. Douglas. *The Human Aura: A Study of Human Energy Fields*. Essenden, UK: Dr. Douglas Baker, 1986.

Bendit. Lawrence J. and Phoebe D. Bendit. *The Etheric Body of Man*. Wheaton, IL: The Theosophical Publishing House, 1977. (First published 1957 as *Man Incarnate*.)

Birren, Faber. *The Symbolism of Color*. Secaucus, NJ: Citadel Press, 1988.

Chiazzari, Suzy. *Colour Scents: Healing with Colour and Aroma*. Saffron Walden, UK: The C. W. Daniel Company Limited, 1998.

———. *The Complete Book of Colour*. Shaftesbury, UK: Element Books Limited, 1998.

Chocron, Daya Sarai. *Healing the Heart: Opening and Healing the Heart with Crystals and Gemstones*. York Beach, ME: Samuel Weiser, Inc., 1989.

Coates, Margrit. *Hands-on Healing for Pets: The Animal Lover's Essential Guide to Using Healing Energy*. London: Rider & Company, 2003.

Dale, Cyndi. *New Chakra Healing*. St. Paul, MN: Llewellyn Publications, 1996.

Hansen, Bente. *The New World of Self-Healing: Awakening the Chakras and Rejuvenating Your Energy Field*. Woodbury, MN: Llewellyn Publications, 2006.

Judith, Anodea. *Wheels of Life: A User's Guide to the Chakra System*. St. Paul, MN: Llewellyn Publications, 1987. Second edition 1999.

Kok Sui, Master Choa. *Miracles Through Pranic Healing*. Makati City, Philippines: Institute for Inner Studies, Publishing, 1999. (First edition, *Pranic Healing*, 1990.)

Leadbeater, C. W. *The Chakras*. Wheaton, IL: The Theosophical Publishing House, 1927.

Lingerman, Hal A. *The Healing Energies of Music*. Wheaton, IL: The Theosophical Publishing House, 1983.

Mann, John, and Lar Short. *The Body of Light*. Rutland, VT: Charles E. Tuttle Company, Inc., 1990.

Mumford, Dr. Jonn. *A Chakra & Kundalini Workbook*. St. Paul, MN: Llewellyn Publications, 1994.

Myss, Caroline. *Anatomy of the Spirit*. New York: Harmony Books, 1996.

Oslie, Pamala. *Life Colors: What the Colors in Your Aura Reveal*. Novato, CA: New World Library, 1991. Revised edition, 2000.

Panchadasi, Swami. *The Human Aura: Astral Colors and Thought Forms*. Chicago, IL: Yoga Publication Society, 1912.

Regush, Nicholas (editor). *The Human Aura.* New York: Berkley Publishing Corporation, 1977.

Roberts, Ursula. *The Mystery of the Human Aura.* London: The Spiritualist Association of Great Britain, 1950. Reprinted by Samuel Weiser, Inc., York Beach, ME, 1977. Revised edition 1984.

Slate, Joe H. *Aura Energy for Health, Healing and Balance.* St. Paul, MN: Llewellyn Publications, 1999.

Smith, Mark. *Auras: See Them in Only 60 Seconds.* St. Paul, MN: Llewellyn Publications, 1997.

Walker, Dr Morton. *The Power of Color.* New York: Avery Publishing Group, Inc., 1991.

Webster, Richard. *Aura Reading for Beginners.* St. Paul, MN: Llewellyn Publications, 1998.

———. *Dowsing for Beginners.* St. Paul, MN: Llewellyn Publications, 1996.

———. *Pendulum Magic for Beginners.* St. Paul, MN: Llewellyn Publications, 2002.

Wills, Pauline. *Colour Healing Manual.* London: Judy Piatkus (Publishers) Ltd., 2000.

———. *Colour Reflexology for Health and Wellbeing.* London: Vega, 2002.

NOTES

Introduction

1. Leonard George, *Alternative Realities: The Paranormal, the Mystic and the Transcendant in Human Experience* (New York: Facts on File, Inc., 1995), 24.

2. Paracelsus, quoted in Lewis Spence, *An Encyclopedia of Occultism* (London: George Routledge & Sons Ltd. 1920), 51.

3. Walter J. Kilner, *The Human Atmosphere (The Aura)* (New York: E. P. Dutton & Co., 1920), 262.

4. David Heiserman, quoted in *The Schlieren System—An Aura Detector?* by Sheila Ostrander and Lynn Schroeder, article in *The Human Aura*, edited by Nicholas Regush (New York: Berkley Books, 1977), 190.

5. *The Schlieren System—An Aura Detector?* by Sheila Ostrander and Lynn Schroeder, article in *The Human Aura*, edited by Nicholas Regush, 190.

6. Sheila Ostrander and Lynn Schroeder, *Psychic Discoveries Behind the Iron Curtain* (New York: Bantam Books, 1970), 203–207.

7. Valerie V. Hunt, *Infinite Mind: Science of the Human Vibrations of Consciousness* (Malibu, CA: Malibu Publishing Company, 1989. Revised edition 1996).

8. Thelma Moss, *The Body Electric: A Personal Journey into the Mysteries of Parapsychology and Kirlian Photography* (Los Angeles: J. P. Tarcher, 1979), 143–149.

9. Harry Oldfield and Roger Coghill, *The Dark Side of the Brain: Major Discoveries in the Use of Kirlian Photography and Electrocrystal Therapy* (Dorset, UK: Element Books, 1988). Grant Solomon and Jane Solomon, *Harry Oldfield's Invisible Universe: The Story of One Man's Search for the Healing Methods that will Help Us Survive the 21st Century* (Wellingborough, UK: Thorsons Publishers, 1998. Revised edition, 2003).

10. Masaki Kobayashi, Daisuke Kikuchi and Hitoshi Okamura, *Imaging of Ultraweak Spontaneous Photon Emission from Human Body Displaying Diurnal Rhythm*. Article in online journal PloS ONE, July 16, 2009. http://www.pubmed central.nih.gov/articlerender.fcgi?tool=pubmed&pubme did=19606225

Chapter One

1. Ursula Roberts, *The Mystery of the Human Aura* (London: The Spiritualist Association of Great Britain, 1950), 1.

2. Swami Panchadasi, *The Human Aura: Astral Colors and Thought Forms* (Chicago: Yoga Publication Society, 1912), 6. Swami Panchadasi was one of many pseudonyms used by William Walker Atkinson (1862-1932). There are several editions of this book available free of charge on the Internet.

3. Cassandra Eason, *Encyclopedia of Magic & Ancient Wisdom* (London: Judy Piatkus (Publishers) Limited, 2000), 11.

4. Ursula Roberts, *The Mystery of the Human Aura.* (York Beach, ME: Samuel Weiser, Inc., revised edition 1984), 7. (Originally published by The Spiritualist Association of Great Britain, London, in 1950.)

Chapter Two

1. Richard Webster, *Dowsing for Beginners* (St. Paul, MN: Llewellyn Publications, 1996), xiii.

2. Dr. Charles T. Tart, *The Scientific Study of the Human Aura.* Article in *The Human Aura*, edited by Nicholas Regush (New York: Berkley Books, 1977), 145–150.

Chapter Three

1. Helen Varley (editor), *Colour* (London: Marshall Editions Limited, 1980), 44.

2. Edvard Munch, quoted in Robert Hughes, *Nothing if Not Critical: Selected Essays on Art and Artists* (London: Penguin Books, 1991), 285.

Chapter Four

1. Richard Gerber, M.D., *Vibrational Medicine* (Santa Fe: Bear and Company Publishing, 1988), 132.

2. Dr. Horoshi Motoyama and R. Brown, *Science and the Evolution of Consciousness: Chakras, Ki, and Psi* (Brookline: Autumn Press, Inc., 1978), 93–98.

3. Dr. Valerie Hunt, *Electronic Evidence of Auras, Chakras in UCLA Study.* Article in *Brain/Mind Bulletin*, Vol. 3, No. 9 (March 20, 1978). Dr. Hunt found that the normal frequencies of brain waves were between 0 and 100 cycles per second. Muscle frequency was up to 225 cps, and the heart 250 cps.

However, the readings over the chakras varied in a range of frequencies between 100 and 1600 cps.

4. Bill Whitcomb, *The Magician's Companion* (St. Paul, MN: Llewellyn Publications, 1993), 101.

5. Alice A. Bailey, *The Soul and its Mechanism* (New York: Lucis Publishing Company, 1930), 119.

6. Denise Whichello Brown, *The Crystals Handbook* (Bideford, UK: D & S Books Ltd., 2007), 23.

Chapter Seven

1. Helen Varley (editor), *Colour* (London: Marshall Editions Limited, 1980), 46.

2. Seth Pancoast, *Blue and Red Lights* (Philadelphia: J. M. Stoddart & Company, 1877), 25.

3. Edwin D. Babbitt, *The Principles of Light and Color* (Orange, NJ: Edwin D. Babbitt, 1878, revised edition 1896).

4. Dinshah P. Ghadiali, *Spectro-Chrome Metry Encyclopedia* (Malago, NJ: Spectro-Chrome Institute, 1934).

5. Jacob Liberman, *Light: Medicine of the Future* (Santa Fe: Bear & Company, 1991).

6. Dr. Morton Walker, *The Power of Color* (New York: Avery Publishing Group, 1991), 79–80.

7. Dr. Morton Walker, *The Power of Color*, 83–84.

8. S. M. Wright, *Validity of the Human Energy Field Assessment Form*. Article in *Western Journal of Nursing Research* 13 (5) (Thousand Oaks, CA: Sage Publications, 1991), 635–647.

Chapter Nine

1. Hal A. Lingerman, *The Healing Energies of Music* (Wheaton, IL: The Theosophical Publishing House, 1983), 14.

Chapter Eleven

1. The brachial chakra was discovered by the internationally known, English animal healer, Margrit Coates, author of *Hands-on Healing for Pets: The Animal Lover's Essential Guide to Using Healing Energy* (London: Rider & Company, 2003). Her website is: www.theanimalhealer.com.

INDEX

BACH FLOWER REMEDIES FOR BEGINNERS
38 Essences that Heal from Deep Within
DAVID VENNELLS

Here is a system of healing that is natural, powerful, and simple to use. If you can observe someone's state of mind, you can select the appropriate Bach Flower Remedy for that person. Someone who is always impatient and quick in thought, for example, might need Impatiens. Someone who is dreamy and needs a lot of sleep may be a classic Clematis.

Bach Flower Remedies work on the subtle mental and emotional levels of the mind, where illness actually begins. They target the particular negative states of mind that give rise to physical symptoms, thus protecting us from future illness. You do not need a medical background to effectively use these 38 different remedies for yourself, friends, family, even pets.

Many people have also noticed their spiritual lives renewed or reborn as a result of the remedies. This book will show you how to use these remedies immediately and safely.

978-0-7387-0047-2
312 pp., 5³⁄₁₆ x 8 $12.95

Spanish Edition:
Flores de Bach para principiantes
978-0-7387-0062-5 $12.95

Reiki for Beginners
Mastering Natural Healing Techniques
David Vennells

Reiki is a simple yet profound system of hands-on healing developed in Japan during the 1800s. Millions of people worldwide have already benefited from its peaceful healing intelligence that transcends cultural and religious boundaries. It can have a profound effect on health and well-being by re-balancing, cleansing, and renewing your internal energy system.

Reiki for Beginners gives you the very basic and practical principles of using Reiki as a simple healing technique, as well as its more deeply spiritual aspects as a tool for personal growth and self-awareness. Unravel your inner mysteries, heal your wounds, and discover your potential for great happiness. Follow the history of Reiki, from founder Dr. Mikao Usui's search for a universal healing technique, to the current development of a global Reiki community. Also included are many new ideas, techniques, advice, philosophies, contemplations, and meditations that you can use to deepen and enhance your practice.

978-1-56718-767-0
336 pp., 5³⁄₁₆ x 8 $13.95

Spanish Edition:
Reiki para principiantes
978-1-56718-768-7 $12.95

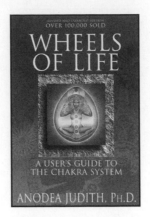

WHEELS OF LIFE
A User's Guide to the Chakra System
ANODEA JUDITH

An instruction manual for owning and operating the inner gears that run the machinery of our lives. Written in a practical, down-to-earth style, this fully illustrated book will take the reader on a journey through aspects of consciousness, from the bodily instincts of survival to the processing of deep thoughts.

Discover this ancient metaphysical system under the new light of popular Western metaphors: quantum physics, Kabbalah, physical exercises, poetic meditations, and visionary art. Learn how to open these centers in yourself, and see how the chakras shed light on the present world crises we face today. And learn what you can do about it!

This book will be a vital resource for: magicians, witches, pagans, mystics, yoga practitioners, martial arts people, psychologists, medical people, and all those who are concerned with holistic growth techniques.

978-0-87542-320-3
528 pp., 6 x 9 $21.95

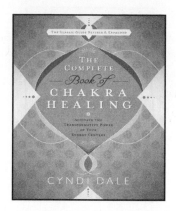

THE COMPLETE BOOK OF CHAKRA HEALING
Activate the Transformative Power of Your Energy Centers
CYNDI DALE

When first published in 1996 (formerly titled: *New Chakra Healing*), Cyndi Dale's guide to the chakras established a new standard for healers, intuitives, and energy workers worldwide. This groundbreaking book quickly became a bestseller. It expanded the seven-chakra system to thirty-two chakras, explained spiritual points available for dynamic change, and outlined the energetic system so anyone could use it for health, prosperity, and happiness.

Presented here for the first time is the updated and expanded edition, now titled *The Complete Book of Chakra Healing*. With nearly 150 more pages than the original book, this groundbreaking edition is poised to become the next classic guide to the chakras. This volume presents a wealth of valuable new material:

- The latest scientific research explaining the subtle energy system and how it creates the physical world
- Depiction of the negative influences that cause disease, as well as ways to deal with them
- Explanations of two dozen energy bodies plus the meridians and their uses for healing and manifesting

978-0-7387-1502-5
456 pp., 7½ x 9⅛ $24.95

CRYSTALS FOR BEGINNERS
A Guide to Collecting & Using Stones & Crystals
CORRINE KENNER

Revered for their beauty, unique electrical qualities, and metaphysical attributes, crystals have been precious to mankind for centuries. *Crystals for Beginners* explores the universal allure of crystals and demonstrates how to channel their dynamic energies.

Beginning with how crystals were formed in the Earth billions of years ago, this practical guide introduces the history and myth surrounding these powerful minerals. From agates to zoisite, the characteristics of specific crystals are presented, along with advice for collecting, cleansing, and charging them. Readers also learn how to apply crystal energy to meditation, healing, psychic development, magic, divination, astral projection, dream work, and much more.

978-0-7387-0755-6
264 pp., 5³⁄₁₆ x 8 $13.95